I dedicate this entire work to my late mother whose soul has been always my inspiration, to my wife who is the source of my force and to my firstborn who has brought much happiness and enthusiasm to our life…..

Hieratic Documents from the Ramesside Period in the Egyptian Museum of Cairo

Abdel Rahman Abdel Samie

GHP Egyptology 14

London 2010

This title is published by
Golden House Publications

Front cover image: ostracon, Cairo, Egyptian Museum, JE 72501 (SR 1516)
Back cover image (top): Cairo Egyptian Museum, JE 72462
Back cover image (bottom): Cairo Egyptian Museum, JE 72466

Printed in the United Kingdom
by

Antony Rowe Limited
Bumper's Farm
Chippenham
Wiltshire SN14 6LH

London 2010

ISBN 978-1-906137-21-2

Contents

Introduction	1
Edition of Texts	3
Interpretation	61
Abbreviations	70
Bibliography	71
Indexes	80
- Index of Deities, Kings, Princes	
- Index of ranking titles	
- Index of personal names	
- Documents quoted	
Facsimile	87

List of illustrations

Illustrative map showing the findspots of ostraca in the Valley of the Kings	64
Illustrative map with records taken from the inventory registers of MMA	65
Illustrative map with huts discovered so far in the Valley of the Kings	66
KVO 1	Pl. I, fig. 1a, b
KVO 2	Pl. II, fig. 2a, b
KVO 3	Pl. III, fig. 3
KVO 4	Pl. IV, fig. 4a, b
KVO 5	Pl. V, fig. 5a, b
KVO 6	Pl. VI, fig. 6
KVO 7	Pl. VII, fig. 7a, b
KVO 8	Pl. VIII, fig. 8a, b
KVO 9	Pl. IX, fig. 9
KVO 10	Pl. X, fig. 10
KVO 11	Pl. XI, fig. 11
KVO 12	Pl. XII, fig. 12a, b
KVO 13	Pl. XIII, fig. 13
KVO 14	Pl. XIV, fig. 14
KVO 15	Pl. XV, fig. 15
KVO 16	Pl. XVI, fig. 16
KVO 17	Pl. XVII, fig. 17
KVO 18	Pl. XVIII, fig. 18
KVO 19	Pl. XIX, fig. 19a, b

Acknowledgments

I am deeply grateful to the great help of Dr. M. Bommas who has granted me the opportunity to pursue this project through an academic place at Birmingham University. I am very appreciated to his scientific guidance which demonstrates that he has saved no effort to direct me all along the course of this work. I am also indebted to the crucial scientific advices of Dr. T. Leahy to polish and enhance the final outcome. I would like also to thank Mrs. Patsy Gasparetti, the English native editor who has kindly revised my English. I should express my gratitude to Dr. W. Grajetzki who has helped me reproduce a digital map of the Valley of the Kings. Special thanks should be addressed to our General Secretary of the Supreme Council of Antiquities, Prof. Dr. Zahy Hawas for his encouragement to curators and inspectors to protect and valorise our patrimony.

INTRODUCTION

As assistant curator in the Egyptian Museum in Cairo, I have been charged to conduct several documentation processes on the unpublished material held by the museum. Prof. Dr. Mamdouh el-Damaty (the former General Director), to whom I remain unable to convey my enormous gratitude to his constant support, had assigned me of the task of compiling an inventory registration of the uncatalogued hieratic ostraca spread throughout all departments of the Egyptian Museum. During the course of my search, it was rapidly revealed that there are great numbers of ostraca spread throughout different departments' storage magazines along with those held in the basement storage area. They are quite diverse in terms of their scripts: hieroglyphic, hieratic, Demotic, Coptic, Greek and Aramaic ostraca. The bulk of these ostraca along with jar labels have never been systematically registered. Of all these unregistered ostraca, the hieratic ones predominate in terms of quantity. I estimate that there are considerably more than 1000 hieratic ostraca left out of a proper scientific treatment, excluding the high number of the same type in the basement. That has prompted me to put this issue on the table for taking serious action.

At the beginning of the last century, G. Daressy had published a major group of hieratic ostraca from the Valley of the Kings, followed by J. Černy, who published another group, the majority of which is also from the Valley of the Kings.

One of the chief reasons to conduct this study is that the ink of a great number of the ostraca has been dramatically effaced. This is a result of the elevated amount of humidity trapped in the Egyptian Museum. Dust mixed with moisture fills in the pores on the surface of a large number of ostraca and causes a dramatic disappearance of ink. The recovery of surviving texts is one of the primary aims of this study. If tangible action towards the salvage and conservation of this material is not expeditiously undertaken, there is a great risk in the nearest future of losing such important data that could well materially contribute to the existing knowledge of the Ramesside Period. The salvage process requires high interest and collaboration from all the concerned parties to document, at a highly scientific level, this material and bring it to the light in order that the ostraca can be systematically documented and returned to public display in the Egyptian Museum. Egyptian and international visitors alike would then be afforded the opportunity of seeing completely unknown material that has been long excluded from public viewing. Therefore, it is not only in the interests of the Egyptian Supreme Council of Antiquities to bring this unknown material to light but there also is likewise a broader, international need for documenting these objects, their data is in a state of great precariousness.

For the information of the reader, we have amended the original corpus of ostraca selected for the MPhil degree to reformulate them for this publication.

This monograph is considered a part of a more extensive documentation process on the entire corpus of hieratic ostraca held in Cairo Museum. For the sake of undertaking proper registration on this set of ostraca, we have selected 19 texts (ostraca and jar labels), their ink is notably effacing. These ostraca and jar labels in question come from the Valley of the Kings; they were discovered by Davis and Carter/Carnarvon. They contain diverse accounts which concern mostly day-to-day journal.

Special thanks should be addressed to Černy as his work been an indispensable reference for any scholar who may seek to work on Ramesside hieratic documents.

The catalogue part of this study (Edition of Texts) occupies the major part of this dissertation in terms of size. Each item (ostracon or jar label) has been exposed with picture, facsimile and transcription; a detailed commentary accompanied with some philological aspects on the terminology used by scribes was integrated as well. In the major part of this process, our endeavour was mostly concentrated to place each ostracon within its cultrual framework. Where personal names are mentioned, an attempt of drawing interconnecting relations has been produced in form of prosopographical study to date some roughly undatable ostraca. A detailed study (classification) has also been drawn on some ostraca in search for getting more insight into their contents.

As far as the archaeological context is concerned, the "Interpretation Chapter" has come to recontextualize Davis' excavations. My target was to systemize some of the misconceptions associated with his records and to attempt identifying the location of some ostraca with unknown provenance.

For convenience, we have set up some catalogue conventions to facilitate the reading. They are as follows:

KVO is the abbreviation of Kings Valley Ostracon.

O. Ashm is the abbreviation of O. Ashmolean Museum as it has occurred frequently

[ ] indicates some lost parts which have been restored by us

[…] means missing group of hieroglyphs

In the transcription part, impossible reading is referred to with ; in the transliteration part by (?)

The facsimile have not been reproduced on 1:1 scale for publication purposes. The exact measurements of each ostracon have been cited in the main text of this monograph.

At last, all uncertainties of language and content remain my own responsibility.

EDITION OF TEXTS

KVO 1 (Pl. I; fig. 1a,b)
O. Cairo JE 72461 (SR 1476)
A list of absentee workmen?

Transliteration (*recto a*);

(1) *š3d* [...]
(2) *Nḫt-sw*[a] *Ḫ*ʿ[...]
(3) *Ḳn-ḥr-ḫpš.f*[b] (*?*) [...]
(4) *b3kw*[c] *p3* [...]
(5) (*Ḥs)i-sw-nb.f*[d]
(6) [...] (*?*) *prt sw 7* [...]

Translation (*recto* a)

(1) dig [...]
(2) *Nḫt-sw* (and) *Ḫ*ʿ[...]
(3) *Ḳn-ḥr-ḫpš.f* (*?*) [...]
(4) the work of [...]
(5) (*Ḥs)i-sw-nb.f* [...]
(6) [...] (?) the Growing season, day 7 [...]

Transliteration (*recto* b)

(1) [...] *3ḫt sw 4*[...]
(2) [...] [*?*] *ḥsb.t-rnp.t 6 ḳ*(*?*) [...]
(3) [...] *n* ʿ*3 n is.t*[e] *Ḥ3y*[f][...]
(4) *n m*ʿ ʿ*3 is.t*

Translation (*recto* b)

(1) [...] the inundation season [...]
(2) [...] regnal year 6 [...]
(3) [...] of the chief of the gang "*Ḥ3y*" [...]
(4) [...] together with the chief of the gang

Transliteration (*verso* a)

(1) *ḥry Ḫ*ʿ *–m-nwn*[g] [...]
(2) [...] (?) *3bd 3 prt sw 8 P3-imi-r-iḫ.w*[h] [...]
(3) [...] [*Ḥwy*] *s3 Ḥwy-nfr*[i] *wsf*
(4) [...] [*Ḥrw-m-wi3*[j]] *ḥr* (*?*) [...]
(5)

Translation (*verso a*)

(1) The superior *Ḫ*ʿ *–m-nwn* [...]
(2) [...] (?) the third month of the Growing season, the 8th day, "*P3-mr-iḫw*"
(3) [...][*Ḥwy*] son of "*Ḥwy-nfr*" is absent [...]
(4) [...] [*Ḥrw-m-wi3*] will on (?) [...]

Transliteration (*verso* b)

(1) (*?*)
(2) [...] *Ḫnm-m-sw*[k] [...]
(3) [...] *3bd* (*?*) *prt sw 12*[...]

Translation (*verso* b)

(1) (?)
(2) [...] *Ḫnm-m-sw* [...]
(3) [...] month (?) of the Growing season, day 12 [...]

Commentary

- Dimension: a, 5.5 x 4 cm and b, 4 x 3.5 cm.
- Material: Limestone.
- Provenance: Valley of the Kings (Davis' excavations).
- Cft. Černy's MSS (106- 12f), transcription only.
- Dating: According to the Special Register[1], it can date to the end of XIXth dynasty.
- Condition: the ostracon is in a good condition with some chipped off parts. Most probably, both parts (a, b) constituted a larger ostracon. The ostracon is written in a black ink which is legible throughout the entire ostracon. In some parts of KVO 1, a", the writing is slightly fading but it can still be drawn up without a significant effort. It is mottled with rounded black stains in its upper and lower part. With regard to part "b *recto*", the ink is in a better condition in respect with that of "a *recto*". However, it is dappled with more remarkable black points, spread sparsely, which are a result of inappropriate storage habits. That can render the reading process slightly hard as these black dots may shape-shift with some hieratic signs and then cause some misreading. The *verso* "a" is slightly worse in terms of state as its writing is distinctly fading and some lines have completely effaced (ex. line 4). As for *verso* "b", the second line is hardly legible either because of the damage or because of the disappearance of the ink.
- Description: With regard to the "*recto* a", it is inscribed in 6 lines; however the *verso* is composed of only 3 lines. These two pieces had been reassembled together because it was thought that they constituted one larger single ostracon. The edges of the two parts (a, b) are notably chipped off. However, the left side border of "*recto* a" is more flaked off than the other one. As a result, there are some signs which are hardly reconstructable, especially in lines (3, 6). The same can be applied to "*recto* b" lines (2, 3) as it sounds that some signs became completely obscure or totally erased with the flaking process. As for "*verso* a", there are 4 inscribed lines with black ink. In contrast to the first two lines, the last two lines are obviously vanishing, especially in line "4". However, "*verso* b" is still relatively in a better condition in spite of the damage of the third line. Moreover, line "1" is entirely erased and there still remains merely an unreadable black dot.

a. "*Nḫt-sw*"[2] written is the "servant of the Lord of the Two Lands in the Place of the Truth".[3] It is thought that there are two monuments testifying the existence of this member of the crew of the left side. However, this ostracon can be considered as a testimony for the occurrence of his name for the third time. The first attestation for his name is dated year 1 of Amenmesse, however his span of time could have started off during the reign of king , ; the final attestation to his name is dated year 5 of king Siptah.[4] The name after "*Nḫt-sw*" starts off with *Ḫ*ʿ which can be hardly reconstructed as there were many workmen whose names have *Ḫ*ʿ as prefix.

b. *Ḳn-ḥr-ḫpš.f* could be identified with that workman who appeared mostly in a number of ostraca dated to the end of the XIXth dynasty (O. Cairo CG 25521, O. Cairo CG 25783, O. DeM 290).

c. "*b3kw*" is a very common word which is characteristic of the Deir El-Medina and Valley of the Kings' terminology. It appeared on a very wide range of ostraca (O. Cairo CG 25237, O. DeM 10097, 25264….etc) with meaning work, project, toil, or output.[5] In this context, it would be best appropriate to be translated as "project", or "work" as a result of the initial word "*š3d*" which means "dig". Unfortunately, the missing part of the ostracon has resulted in obscuring the proper name which is preceded by "*p3*".

---

[1] Cairo Museum inventory register.
[2] RPN II, 211.
[3] Tosi/ Roccati 1972, N. 50041 (= cat. 1454), 75.
[4] Davies 1999, 243 (chart 35).
[5] Lesko & Lesko 1982-1990 I, 146.

d. The initial part of this name is missing. However we may be able to restore it as *Ḥsi-sw-nb.f.* The occurrence of his name might be assigned to the reign of Amenmesse onwards.[6]

e. *ʿ3 n is.t* is the counterpart of the hieroglyphic title (*ḥry is.t*) which means "foreman". (*ʿ3 n is.t*) was very peculiar of the administrative terminology and always in singular form. The genitival "*n*" is seldom omitted. The corrupt O. Toronto B 7, 5 has redundantly .[7]

f. For *Ḥ3y*[8], he could be the foreman whose tenure to the office lasted from year 3 of Merenptah to year 19 of Ramses III. From the records of this title, it was revealed that this title was rather hereditary one which was transferred from a father to his son. In other words, a son of a foreman should have automatically inherited the tenure of his father's office. Moreover, there could be more than foreman contemporary. The appointment of a foreman was not carried out by the vizier but rather by the local administration.[9]

g. For *Ḫʿ-m-nwn*, we know that there were at least four individuals bearing the same name; but according to his title "*ḥry*" which stands before his proper name, we can identify him as the chief of the policemen who was first attested on O. DeM 290, 5.[10] Judging from the names which appeared with him on the same ostracon, we hypothesize that the ostracon in question was probably written in the second half of the XIXth dynasty.

h. As for "*P3-imi-r-iḥ.w*"[11], he can be identified with a workman of the same name who appeared towards the close of the XIXth dynasty.[12]

i. With regard to "*Ḥwy-nfr*", he can be tentatively identified with the sculptor who appeared at the first half of the XIXth dynast.[13] However, the name mentioned on this ostracon is the son of this *Ḥwy-nfr,* who might be the workman "*Ḥwy*". Therefore, we would hint that the dating of this ostracon can be roughly ascribed to the second half of the XIXth dynasty and can probably extend into the XXth dynasty.

j. For *Ḥrw-m-wi3,* according to the general dating framework we have drawn above, this person can be identified with the workman with the same name who received in a year "2" a painted coffin for *Ḫʿ-m-tr*, the chief door-keeper, at the end of the XIXth dynasty.[14]

k. Regarding "*Ḫnm-m-sw*"[15], he can be identified as the "Child of the tomb". This title was held by several families among which there was *Ḫnm-m-sw*'s.[16] His span of time might have extended into the XXth dynasty.[17]

Schematic prosopography:
KVO 1 lists a number of labours who may be safely assigned to the end of the XIXth dynasty. One of these workmen is "*Ḥsi-sw-nb.f*" whose name has been mentioned on some objects that are dated safely to the above indicated period. From these monuments, we may cite the stela erected in the Ramesseum representing him together with another workman called "*Nfr-ḥtp.w*", who might have been his father; this stela is dated to the second half of the XIXth dynasty.[18] On this stela he has the title "the servant of the Lord of the Two Lands in the Place of the Truth", exactly like that of "*Nfr-ḥtp*". The wife of

---

[6] Davies 1999, 229.
[7] Černy 2004, 121.
[8] RPN III, 232.
[9] Černy 2004, 122-132.
[10] Ibid, 268.
[11] RPN II, 100.
[12] Davies 1999, 185; KRI III, 659-660; stela Louvre N. 662 (PM I: II 772) ; his name also has been mentioned on O. DeM 295(I [3]-4) by the sculptor Iyernutef to an unnamed draftsman for the decoration of some item for (*P3*)-*mr-ihw*.
[13] Davies 1999, 18.
[14] Černy 2004, 164.
[15] RPN III, 275.
[16] Černy 2004, 119; Černy & Gardiner 1957, pl. XLIV (6).
[17] Janssen 2005, 47; KRI IV, 330.
[18] Davies 1999 footnote 407.

"*Ḥsi-sw-nb.f*" was involved in a sexual relationship with "*P3-nb*".[19] The former lifetime span extended from the reign of Amenmesse. He might be also the brother-in-law of a certain "*Mry-rꜥ*" who appeared with him in two graffiti in which there is no reference to a term that would determine their relationship.[20] "*Mry-rꜥ*" might possibly have lived down to the reign of Ramses V or VI.[21] We cannot define his exact lifetime span with more certainty though. Another workman's name "*Nḫt-sw*" can be also considered as a vivid clue of dating. The first occurrence of his name may have attested in Merenptah's reign. The final attestation of his name may date to year 5 of Siptah; he first appeared in year 1 of Amenmesse's reign. Thus, we might confine our dating framework between year 1 of Amenmesse and year 5 of Siptah. By virtue of his name, "*P3-imi-r-iḥ.w*", the workman, appeared at the close of the XIXth dynasty. To be more precise, he happened to be, for the first time, in service in year 1 of Siptah. [22] His name is mentioned also on a stela which he dedicated in honour of Queen Ahmes-Nefertari.[23] On this stela, he was assigned to be the "the sculptor in the Place of the Truth". On O. DeM 269, his name has occurred in association with a scribe called "*P3-srw*". There were many scribes bearing the same name, from year 8 of Merenptah down to the middle of the XXth dynasty.[24] That can entitle us to define *P3-mr-iḥ.w*'s working time span, at latest, down into the same time. However, what we are most concerned about is that he first appeared sometime during the first years of Siptah's reign. On these grounds, the date of the ostracon in question may more precisely be confined between year 1 and year 5 of Siptah. The breakthrough evidence is the mention of the regnal year 6, which could be a decisive evidence to attribute KVO 1 to year 6 of Siptah's reign. On the other hand, it is hard to determine the time span of the "Superior *Ḫꜥ-m-nwn*" as the use of the word "*ḥry*" renders his name too difficult to identify. He has probably been mentioned on an ostracon (O. DeM 290, vso. 5) dated to the end of the XIXth dynasty, as the "Chief of the *mḏ3y*".[25] Černy has suggested about a certain "*Ḫꜥ-m-nwn*", that he lived, holding tenure of the office of the Chief of "*mḏ3y*", during the second half of Ramses II's reign. We would not be able to venture to hypothesise that they might have been the same person, although we cannot rule out that completely. In another ostracon (O. BM EA 50730 + O. BM EA 50745, rto.5), he happened to be the "Chief of the Cattle"; this ostracon is dated year 1 of Ramses VI.[26] We would be inclined to identify him with the "Chief of *mḏ3y*", relying on the information provided about him. His name is associated with "*ḥry*" but nothing else. At any rate, we learn that either of the two "*Ḫꜥ-m-nwns*" may have lived down to year 1 of Ramses VI, at latest.

Classification:

KVO 1 initial word starts off with a word which conveys a construction work by the use of word "*š3d*", meaning "dig" or "dig out".[27] After that, there comes a word "*wsf* = off" meaning rather "off" or inactive. For "*š3d*", written [hieroglyphs], it appeared with this meaning as old as the Old Kingdom time, Pepi I's reign, at Akhmim site.[28] The word "*š3d*" can be translated as "dig"; when added to "*inr*", the meaning is "quarry".[29] Unfortunately, the whole line has been fragmented and so has been the whole sentence. Therefore, we cannot venture on hypothesising an exact meaning for this word. Nevertheless, we may be able to infer that there might have been some specific work activity being handled by the workforce mentioned on this ostracon. Accordingly, the ostracon could be classified merely as an account that contains a list of names; some of them were inactive others might have been involved in some working activities, probably related to digging.The same word occurred in (O. DeM

---

[19] Ibid, 65.
[20] Černy & Sadek 1971, 4.
[21] Černy 2004, 353 (footnote 5) .
[22] Davies 1999, 187.
[23] Vienna inv no.158.
[24] Davies 1999, 102.
[25] Collier, 2004, 123-124, 157-158.
[26] KRI VII, 360-61.
[27] Wb 4, 414. 11-415.4.
[28] Kanawati 1986, 49, 51, Pl. 3b, 8c, fig. 20.
[29] Meeks III 1779, 284 (79.2929).

159. 6a, and O. DeM 144 vso.10). If the word was intended to function as “dig” in meaning, then this word might probably imply that the account on *recto* “a” concerns a digging work in some king’s tomb. The same word can be also translated as “Pillage” and written .[30] The determinatives of this word may be the forearm or the forearm with the stick. So, we would be more inclined here to rule out this meaning as the following context is totally irrelevant to the word “pillage”.

As for *wsf*,[31] (time off with permission on certain events like inspection, feasts, doing certain assignments like bringing water and so forth), it can be abbreviated in such designation when there is a genitival structure with *tꜣ is.t*.[32] So, there might have been *tꜣ ist* which has been missed out by the fracture of the ostracon. From the content of the two accounts written on either *recto* (a, b) or *verso* (a, b), we can learn that there are not any clues which may correlate them in a common sense. However, the scholar who designated them under one inventory “JE number” might have hinted that they constitute one ostracon. From orthographical perspective, we can notice the resemblance of the handwriting on the two fragments [*recto* (a, b) and *verso* (a, b)]. In addition, the limestone material and the nature of the surface of the two fragments might suggest that they may have constituted a larger ostracon handed down by the same scribe. What is certain about the two fragments is that they contain a day-to-day journal account regarding basically some workmen’s names (probably absence account). Unfortunately, the entire account has been considerably fragmented in a way that the content can hardly be outlined with more certitude.

[30] Lesko & Lesko 1982-1990 III, 135.
[31] O. DeM 340; O. DeM 353.
[32] O. DeM 894-895; Grandet 2003, 68-69.

KVO 2 (Pl. II; fig. 2a, b)
O. Cairo JE 72462 (SR 1477)
A delivery account

Transliteration

(1) [(?) *nḥḥ*[a]] *mn.t 1 it ḫ3r 5*
(2) [*it m*] *it*[b] *ḫ3r 6ḫ3r 11 n bd.t*
(3) [(?)*ḫ3r ꜥ3*[c] *12*] *mnḏm*[e] *ḫ3r 3*
(4) [*nḳr.w*] *ḫ3r* [*3*] *tm3 ḫ3r 6 šꜥ.t tm3*[e]
(5) [(*tm3*)*mw ḫ3r ꜥn*[f]] (*?*) *tiw.ty ꜥ 2*
(6) [*ḥm.t dbn 2 n*] *ꜥḏ hnw 3*
(7) [*sḏr ḫ3r 1 nḥ*]*ḥ hnw 2 wḥm*[g] *hnw 2*
(8) [...] *20*
(9) [...] *3ḫ.*(*w*)*t*[h]

Translation

(1) [(?) Oil], 1 mn.t jar, 5 khar of grain
(2) [Barely] 6 khar of, emmer 11 khar of
(3) [(?)12 great khar of], basketry 3 khar
(4) [Sieves] [3] khar, 6 khar of mat, fine mat
(5) [Mended (mat)] (?) khar (and) two pairs of sandals,
(6) [Copper or bronze 2 dbn], fresh fat 3 hnw
(7) [Sleeping-mat 1 khar of, oil], 2 hnw from new 2 hnw,
(8) [...] 20
(9) [...] goods

Commentary

- Dimension: 13 x 9.5 cm.
- Material: Limestone.
- Provenance: Valley of the Kings (Davis' excavations).
- Cft. Černy MSS (106-12), transcription only.
- Dating: According to the Special Register, the ostracon could ascribe to XIX-XXth dynasty. However, we may set a more precise span of time, depending on the use of word "*hnw*". It used to appear in texts from the middle of the XIXth dynasty on.[33]
- Condition: In more than one vertical third of the *recto*, from top to bottom, the ink is effaced completely. What remains of the inscription is the left side of the *recto*, its ink is obviously well preserved. The overall state is quite precarious as the ink may evidently disappear in the near future.
- Description: The ostracon is inscribed in black ink on two sides. The *recto* has 9 lines with missing top. As a result of that, the upper parts of some of vertical signs like "𓎛" and "𓆰"signs have been partly cut off. The ends of line 1, 2 are effaced; beginnings of lines 1-9 are effaced as well. The end of line 9 is completely lost. There is some correction done by the scribe in line 2. This is why we are relying here basically on Černy MSS "c106-12" to restore all the missing parts of the ostracon. As regards the *verso,* there is some scribbling with marks written by coal. These signs are dubbed recently "Funny-sings"; these marks are drawn as follows: 𓏊 ,𓇳, ⊥, 𓈖. However what have remained are only the first three signs; the last one is totally effaced.

[a.] "*nḥḥ*" is one of the most important items of the workmen's daily rations; usually it was written 𓎛𓇳𓎛 and sometimes𓅮.[34] It is identified to be "sesame oil" and is one of items, its occurrence in documents

[33] Janssen 1975, 333-36.
[34] Janssen 1975, 330.

was not so frequent in the Valley of the Kings' documents with respect to those of Deir el-Medina. It has been mentioned in a very limited number of citations; ex. in O. Cairo JE 72453 published by Helck[35], O. Cairo Carnarvon 421 published by Kitchen[36]. On the other hand, in Deir el-Medina its citations in documents are in numerous quantities. For example, it can be found in O. Turin N. 57366[37], O. DeM 773[38], O. DeM 10102[39], 10044[40], 10082[41], O. DeM 929[42], 930[43], 935.[44] Sometimes the quantity of the "*nḥḥ* oil" could be indicated by the "*mn.t* jar" like the ostracon in question.

b. In ostraca and papyri, when real barely is meant, and not barely as a unit of value, the word is written *it-m-it* (barely as barely).[45] The unit used for measuring is the khar.

c. "*ẖ3r ʿ3*" may probably mean a dozen of khar as the number followed is "12". If "ʿ3" was commonly understood as a "dozen" in meaning, why the scribe did have to cite number 12 then? In fact, there is no any parallel for this phrase and our suggestion here is just based on a pure logic.

d. The word "*mnḏm*" means basketry and is usually associated with word "*nḳr*". The latter could probably signify the lid of the former.[46] In fact, in this ostracon, we notice that the number is the same "3" being associated with the both words. That may strengthen Helck's suggestion when he supposed that there is always association in functioning between them.

e. For "*šmʿ.t tm3*", is a common object in every ancient Egyptian household this is why it is frequently mentioned in texts.[47] The word "*tm3*" was associated with word "*šmʿ*" as just an adjective to qualify the mat as fine.[48] The "*t*" added as a final sign is odd and there is no any explanation for its existence. It could be just a handwriting mistake committed by the scribe. This could be a plausible suggestion as we can see that there is a correction in line 2 which means that the scribe could have probably been haste in writing down this document.

f "*ʿn*" is the adjective which used to qualify the type of the mat. It appeared with many determinatives among which there is also 𓁹.[49] Janssen in "Commodity Prices" has translated this word as either "ornamented" (because of the eye determinative) or "mended". He rather proposes the meaning "mended" which may probably best fit the "mat".

g. "*wḥm*" (Wb 1, 340-343.15; 351.11) means "from new" or "again". It has been used in this context to convey that the quantity of oil has been doubled as first they mentioned "*hnw 2*" and after that "*wḥm hnw 2*" citing the same quantity twice. Or it could probably be just a more emphasized meaning to the same quantity.

h. "*3ẖ.(w)t*" could be translated as "goods".[50]

---

[35] Helck 2002, 142-143, 144-145 (translation); description and transcription in Černý MSS, 106.4.

[36] KRI VII, 253 (transcription); Černy MSS, 14.37.

[37] López 1978-1984 III, 22 (description), pl. 113-113a (facsimile, transcription); López 1978-1984 IV, pl. 204 (photograph); Helck 2002, 455 (translation) ; Janssen 1992, 107-122 and pl. 2 (transcription, translation, commentary); McDowell 1999, 221-222 no. 171 (translation).

[38] Grandet 2000, 53-54 (transiletration and commentary), 178 (photo and facsimile); Černy MSS, 17.116, f° 17.

[39] Grandet 2006, 105 (transliteration and commentary), 301 (photo and facsimile).

[40] Ibid, 49 (transliteration and commentary), 239 (photo and facsimile).

[41] Ibid, 83-84 (transliteration and commentary), 271-274 (photo and facsimile).

[42] Grandet 2003, 104 (transliteration and commentary), 365 (photo and facsimile).

[43] Ibid, 105 (transliteration and commentary), 367 (photo and facsimile).

[44] Ibid, 109 (transliteration and commentary), 372 (photo and facsimile).

[45] Janssen 1975, 119.

[46] Helck 1965, 917.

[47] Janssen 1975, 154.

[48] Examples for that is in O. DeM 772 published in Grandet 2000, 53 (transliteration and commentary).

[49] Janssen 1975, 155.

[50] Lesko & Lesko 1982-1990 I, 9.

KVO 3 (Pl. III; fig. 3)
O. Cairo JE 72463 (SR 1478)
A delivery account + A letter

Transliteration

(1) [...] (?) *s* [...]
(2) [...] *rdy.t* [a] *r s* (?) [...]
(3) [...] *šmw sw 15*(?) [...]
(4) *d* […] *n ḫbs*[b]
(5) *rdi.t n* (?) *r p3 rˁ -b3k,*[c]
(6) *ḫbs* […] *iw.i ḥr*[d] *ḏd n.f iw.k*
(7) *m*[e] *ḫ3ˁ.w m iḫ n3 ḫbsw* […] *iw.f*
(8) *m ḏd n.i msb*[f] *m ḫbs*
(9) [...]

Translation

(1) [...] (?) [...]
(2) [...] what was given to (?) [...]
(3) [...] the inundation season, day 15 (?) [...]
(4) (?) […] lamps
(5) What was given by (?) to the work.
(6) was lamps […], (and) I said to him, you
(7) abandoned them (and) what (about) the lamps? He
(8) said to me that (he) turned toward the lamps
(9) [...]

Commentary

- Dimension: 9 x 9 cm.
- Material: Limestone.
- Provenance: Valley of the Kings (Davis'ecavations).
- Cft. Černy's MSS (106-13f), transcription only.
- Dating: According to the Special Register, it can date to the end of XIXth dynasty. For KVO 3, it regards a delivery account of some lamps along with a letter. Unfortunately, in the letter, neither the name of sender nor that of the addressee is mentioned. Above all, there is no even a single clue for dating, rendering the dating process quite hard to define. Surprisingly, it is attributed to the XIXth dynasty as shown above. We are not in a position either to concede or to deny this attribution. The scholar who has drawn up this date (prehaps Černy) probably had some evidence in hands regarding this ostracon. Unfortunately, this clue is not mentioned anywhere.
- Condition*:* It is broken into four pieces, and has nine lines written in black ink. The writing is legible enough across the ostracon, in spite of the fractures.
- Description: the ostracon is inscribed only on one side and is consisted of nine lines divided into two groups; one upper group has four lines, the other one holds 5 longer line in size. There is a notable space between the upper and the lower group. That can be accounted, as explained later on, for the existence of two different accounts. The ostracon is slightly sharp in its upper part and smashed on the both sides in such a way that those left and right inscriptions are now missing. As a result of that, we can barely extract few hieratic signs. These missing parts on the both sides can continue down to line 3. However, line four is missing some signs only on its left side.

(a) "*rdy.t* + *n* + giver A, noun or pronoun + *r* or *n* + receiver B" is typical administrative expression which occurred commonly in working sites during the Ramesside period. This expression is widely translated as "what was given by A to B or what A gave to B".[51] It can also manifest as *rdy.t n.f m NN* which means "given to him from NN"as it is on O. Aberdeen 1317, published by Allam.[52] Moreover, here "*rdy.t*" can be identified as a passive participle which is best translated in English as "given" and "*n*" is that particle which introduces agents. The passive participle was not often used in written texts and is very restricted in number of verbs; for instance *iri* "do", *rdi* "give", *ini* "fetch", and *gmi* "find" are the most common ones.[53] There was no particular distinction in gender neither number when it took place in a text.[54] In some cases, it could be introduced by a prothetic "yod" which disappears after an article. However, in respect to the active participle, the "yod" occurs less often. In other cases, there could be a prothetic "*r*" with other verbs. Some passive participles have termination which was liable to be replaced by in some occurrences.[55] The passive participle was employed in statements, like [56] *rdy.t n n3 sšw nty ḏdḥ.tw t n wnm 3,* which means "what was given to the scribes who are imprisoned, three loaves for eating".[57]

(b) As what regards *ḫbs* meaning "lamp", it is written "" in (Wb 3, 230.3). It occurs in some letters written on some ostraca, like O. Toronto A11 (vs. line 11)[58], and O. BM 65933 (O. Nash 11)[59] "line [A. vs. 8]". Such word has occurred in a considerable number (around 88 ostraca holding various accounts).[60] On the basis of these sources, it suggests that some of the entries made in a larger tomb (e.g lamp) account may have come from notes taken on smaller ostraca which were then integrated into the large account.[61] In our case, this ostracon might have been that draft of a larger account which may probably have been transferred onto a larger one.

(c) "*p3- rꜥ-b3kw*" could mean (project, work at king's tomb, workers, work).[62] Gardiner translated it as "project".[63] Černy translated it in Salt 124 as "work at pharaoh's tomb". [64] Furthermore, Gardiner translated it as "work" with an additional "*w*" along with a papyrus roll before the standing leaning man, holding the stick by his two hands ().[65] It is difficult favouring one of these translations to the other as all of them can fit in the content.

(d) The construction *iw* + noun or pronoun+ *ḥr* + infinitive is a circumstantial one, composed of the "present 1" (noun + *ḥr* + infinitive). In "present 1" sentences, there should be subject followed by an adverbial predicate (a true adverb, prepositional phrase, *ḥr* + infinitive, *m* + infinitive "verbs of motion only" or pseudo-participle form.[66] The fact that there is *iw* renders the whole clause "*iw.i ḏd n.f*" to be rather translated in concomitance (the major part of present 1) with the preceding

---

[51] O Glasgow D. 1925. 89 (I, 2 and II, 1), published in McDowell 1993, 30 (translation and discussion), pl. XXXI- XXXIa (facsimile and transcription). Other occurrences can be found on O Glasgow D. 1925. 78 (*verso*, 3).
[52] Allam 1973, 17 no. 1 (translation and commentary).
[53] Neveu 1998, 142.
[54] Černy & Israelit Groll 1984, 463-464.
[55] Ibid, 474.
[56] P. Leyde 1350, v°, col III, 11-12 (=KRI II, 810, 1-2).
[57] Neveu 1998, 144.
[58] E. Wente1990, 46 f; KRI III, 43-44; KRI translation III, 30. It is a letter from "*Iny-ḥr.t-ḫ3w*" to a vizier called Khay during the Ramesside Period, Ramses II.
[59] Ibid, 50. It is a letter to a vizier called Hay.
[60] http://www.leidenuniv.nl/nino/dmd/dmd.html.
[61] Donker van Heel & Haring 2003, 44.
[62] Lesko & Lesko 1982-1990 II, 47.
[63] Gardiner 1932, IX, L11.
[64] Černy1929, 249.
[65] Gardiner 1932, II, 2,7.
[66] Neveu 1998, 68.

sentence.[67]Since the sentence preceded was probably "what was given by the high official to "*P3-rꜥ*", we may be inclined to translate this clause in past tense too. So the clause is best translated as "I said to him".

(e) The second present tense construction is composed of "*iw.k m ḫ3ꜥ*" which should be also translated in past tense. Since the "*ḫ3ꜥ*" is a verb of motion in its nature, it has been terminated by the two legs determinative"𓂻". What may be enigmatic is that even the following verb *ḏd* is preceded, according to the transcription, by *m*. This can be probably explained as just an error committed by the scribe as *ḏd* has never been identified as verb of motion.

(f) "*msb*" is very rare verb and has been always a question to debate (Wb 2, 143.11-12-13, 14-16). "*msb*" written 𓄟𓋴𓃀𓂻𓏥 could be a noun with unknown meaning. However, there are diverse derivatives transliterated slightly different; an example for that is *msbb* "𓄟𓋴𓃀𓃀𓀁" which is rendered as verb and means "turn toward" [Wb 2, 143.12-13; vgl. FCD 117 and P. H 500 (pl.18) 10]. If translated so, it will justify the existence of the two legs as determinative "𓂻" as the meaning conveys motion. However, I would like to bring the attention to the 𓆛, the oxyrhynchus fish which is mounting two legs determinative "𓂻".[68] In fact, this word *msb* never appeared with these two determinatives before, rendering this hint somewhat problematic.[69]

Classification:

KVO 3 holds two types of accounts (the upper four lines bear a delivery account of lamps and the lower five ones concern a sort of letter of complaint arising from this delivery). Therefore, the ostracon has been divided spatially to receive two different accounts in nature. For the delivery of lamps, it is shown in some terminology like *rdy.t* (given) and *šmw sw 15* which used to designate such a type of accounts. They are characterized as just a record of item (s)/amounts delivered, often with date and /or person responsible for delivery or receipt.[70] In accordance with that, in the upper part there is mentioned *rdy.t* as well as some traces of the name of the receiver starting with hieroglyph "*s*" and being preceded by "*r*" (to). The lower account is too hard to determine. First time I ever saw this ostracon, it seemed to classify rather as deposition type. That has been demonstrated by the use of the narrative formula which is shown by the use of "*iw*" throughout the text. For instance, *iw.i ḥr ḏd*, and *iw.f m ḏd n.i* are typical expressions used in such content (cft. O. Ashm 36, O. Ashm 254). With regard to the content of this part, it seems that someone was accused of neglecting some lamps given to him by a certain high ranking official whose name is unfortunately missing in this ostracon. In fact, we get an immediate impresion, while reading, that there might have been probably a course of interrogation between two persons; of course an interrogator and an interrogated one. However, according to the general formulae used in ostraca designated as deposition we may be slightly reluctant of attributing it to this typology; the most common formulae used are (*ir ink*), (*sḏm r n NN*), (*ḏd* (*.t*)*.n NN*) which practically have nothing to do with what we are encountering here.[71]On the other hand, we may be more inclined to subcategorize the lower part of this ostracon under report typology (cft. O. Cairo CG 25742,[72]and O. Turin N. 57381[73]). Such type is commonly identified as a narrative text recording one or more event, mentioning dates and some officials. Perhaps, it was just an audit undertaken by a high official to certain lamps which were damaged or lost somewhere. Furthermore, I think that this ostracon may have been a draft for a larger account destined to be sent to the vizier's office.

---

[67] Ibid, 162.
[68] Möller 1927 II, 23.
[69]Lesko & Lesko 1982-1990 I, 241.
[70] O. Ashm 160, published in KRI VII, 362-363 (transcription); Helck 2002, 442 (outline of content). Other instances can be found in O. Ashm 266-270, and O. Cairo CG 25247, 25257.
[71] Donker van Heel & Haring 2003, 167.
[72] Černy 1935a, 75, 89*, pl. XC (description, transcription, facsimile).
[73] López 1978-1984 III, 27, pl. 119-119a.

Alternatively, we may be entitled not rule out completely the probability of ascribing it to "letter" category which has a subtle difference with the "report" one. It looks more like a letter of complaint being sent to high authority for a dispute event which took place in the Valley of the Kings between two parties. The lack of the citation of regnal years along with the unwritten ruling contemporary king's name makes this ascription somewhat doubtful. Nevertheless, we are rather inclined to favour this assumption. There remains one intriguing question which may assert itself at this point; is it normal to get two different accounts attested on one ostracon? In effect, this is not the first time we encounter such melange (administrative account plus deposition) on one ostracon. It is a very common peculiarity either in Deir- el- Medina or in Valley of the Kings' written documents.[74]

[74] O. Ashm 285 published in Valbelle 1977a, 101 (description), pl. 39-39a (facsimile and transcription). Other analogies can be found in O. Cairo CG 25258 and O. DeM 93.

KVO 4 (Pl. IV; fig. 4a, b)
O. Cairo JE 72464 (SR 1479)
A delivery account?

Transliteration (*recto*)

(1) *ir*[a] *tꜣ wꜥ ri.t*[b] *n ist 300* [...]
(2) *ir tꜣ ri.t 30*[...]
(3) *ir* [*Pꜣ 10 ꜣbd*] *ḫꜣr 60*[...]

Translation (*recto)*

(1) As for the side and the other side of the gang, (it is) 300 [...]
(2) As for the side number "2", (they are) 30 [...]
(3) As for [the 10 (?) month], (they are) 60 khar [...]

Transliteration (*verso*)

(1) *ꜣbd 4 prt sw15Ḥwy*[c] *mḥ* [*14*]
(2) *Rꜥ-mry*[d] *mḥ 14* [*ꜣbd 4*]

Translation (*verso)*

(1) Month 4 of the Growing season, day 15 "*Ḥwy*", [the fourteenth (?)]
(2) "*Rꜥ-mry*", the fourteenth (day) [month 4]

Commentary

- Dimension: 12.5 x 14 cm.
- Material: Limestone.
- Provenance: Valley of the Kings (Davis' excavations).
- Cft. Černy's MSS "(106-13), transcription only.
- Dating: According to the Special Register, it can date to XIX- XXth dynasty.
- Condition: It is broken into two pieces. The ink of the *recto* is obviously disappearing especially in line 2, exactly on its very left side. Line 3, however, is completely effaced except the initial word "*ir*", it is slightly more visible in respect with the rest of the line. . With regard to the *verso*, line 1 is entirely effacing; however line 2 is slightly more preserved. It seems that the account was larger but the ostracon had been chipped off, causing an obvious fragmentation to the whole content.
- Description: The *recto* is inscribed with black ink and is consisted of three lines. It sounds that the scribe wanted to stress on the initial word "*ir*" with writing it in a magnified size in comparison to the rest of the words. The writing is clear to read in most of its part. However, the effacing parts are so hard to reconstruct. Therefore, we have relied basically on Černy's MSS to restore these missing parts of writing. The ostracon was chipped off on its left side which caused to disappear some parts of the writing. As for the *verso,* it is written in two lines with minor size and presumably by the same scribe.

[a.] The construction *ir* + noun (or equivalent) / independent form (verbal or not) is used as a theme marker or introducing a topic / rheum = commentary. The whole construction is best translated in English "as for".[75]
[b.] The word "*ri.t*" can be found in (Wb2, 400, 4-13). According to Wb, This word means a part of something and is mostly associated with the definite article "*t3*". In some cases, it can come with "*wꜤ*" and means "the one and the other one of something". In the ostracon in question, there is indirect genitival construction with word "*is.t*" by the use of the genitive particle "n". As for *t3 ri.t,* it has been translated as "side, bank" in Gaballah, Mose and Caminos, Tale.[76] Valbelle, however translated it as "team" in Poids.[77]
[c.] For "*Ḥwy*", it is too hard to identify him precisely as there were many workmen bearing this name.
[d.] In fact, there were many individuals who bore this name but we may probably assign him to a certain "*RꜤ-mry*" who could be identified with the scribe, the son of the workman and magician *Ỉmn-ms*. He lived about the middle of the reign of Ramses II and appeared in connexion with various supplies along with the scribe "*Ỉmn-m-ipt*" in two ostraca dated year 35 of the same king.[78]

Schematic prosopography:
"*Mry-rꜤ*" or "*RꜤ-mry*" can probably be identified with either the workman who lived during the second half of the XXth dynasty or the *smdt* scribe who was known to be active in years 35 and 37 of Ramses II's reign. The fact that there is no office affiliation on this ostracon makes it hard to decide. On the other hand, we cannot rule out the possibility of identifying him with the brother-in-law of "*Ḥsi-sw-nb.f*" who was mentioned in two graffiti and was active by the end of the XIXth dynasty. Grandet states that his time span can be traced from the XIXth dynasty down to year 24 of Ramses III's reign.[79] On these grounds, we would be rather discreet to concur with the broad dating framework given in the inventory register of Cairo Museum (XIX–XXth dynasty).

Classification:
The account is too obscure to get a clear picture of it. Encountering some numbers, dates along with some personal names would suggest that this account is a day-to-day journal. Alternatively, the account could be classified also as a delivery as for the mentioning of word "[hieroglyph]" "*ẖ3r*" followed by number "60". In conclusion, we think that the whole account could be considered as merely a registration of workmen with delivered rations.

---

[75] Neveu 1998, 173.
[76] Caminos 1977, 36, pl 8.4; Gaballah 1977, pl LXI.
[77] Valbelle 1977a, no. 5265.
[78] Černy 2004, 210-211.
[79] Grandet 2003, 50.

KVO 5 (Pl. V; fig. 5a, b)
O. Cairo JE 72466 (SR 1481)
A list of workmen's names

Transliteration (*recto*)

[...]	[...] (1)
[...]	[*Wn-nfr*[a]] (*?*) [*Pn-imn*] (2)
[*Ỉmn-m-i*(*pt*)][b]	*Ḫ*ʿ*-m-*[(*ipt*)][c] (3)
[*Nḫt-imn*][d]	*n Ḫnmw-nḫt*[e] (4)
*[Imn-ḫ*ʿ*w*[f] *s3 Ḥ3y*]	*P3-r*ʿ-[*ḥtp*][g] (5)
[*Mn-n*]*3*[h]	*sbk*-[*ms*][i] (6)
Nb-[*imn.t*][j]	[*P3-nḫt-*ʿ*3*][k] (7)
[*Ḫnm*(*w*) *–ms*(*w*)][l]	*Ḥ[wy-nfr*][m] (8)
(*dmd*)[o] *s* [*15*]	*P*[*3-ḥtp*][n] (9)

Translation (*recto*)

[...]	[...] (1)
[...]	[*Wn-nfr*][a] (*?*) [*Pn-imn*] (2)
[*Ỉmn-m-i*(*pt*)]	*Ḫ*ʿ*-m-*[(*ipt*)] (3)
[*Nḫt-imn*]	*n Ḫnmw-nḫt* (4)
*[Imn-ḫ*ʿ*w*[f] *s3 Ḥ3y*]	*P3-r*ʿ-[*ḥtp*] (5)
[*Mn-n*]*3*	*sbk*-[*ms*] (6)
Nb-[*imnt*]	[*P3-nḫt-*ʿ*3*] (7)
[*Ḫnm –ms*]	*Ḥ[wy-nfr*] (8)
(total) men [15]	*P*[*3-htp*] (9)

Transliteration (*verso*)

(1) [*ms*]
(2) [*P3-imi-r-iḥ.w*][p]
(3) [(*?*) *g3*]
(4) [*ii*(*?*)]

Translation (*verso*)

(1) [*ms*]
(2) [*P3-imi-r-iḥ.w*]
(3) [(*?*) *g3*]
(4) [*ii*(*?*)]

Commentary

- Dimension: 11.5 x 9 cm.
- Material: Limestone.
- Provenance: Valley of the Kings (Davis'exacavations).
- Cft. Černy MSS (106-15f), transcription only.
- Dating: The ostracon is attributed to the XIX-XXth dynasty as for the Special Register.
- Condition: for the *recto,* the ostracon is in very bad conditions and most of the ink is dramatically effaced. However, the general state of the stone is still well-preserved. There are two upright fractures, not so profound, which run across the ostracon from top to bottom. On the left side towards the bottom, an almost rounded piece is chipped off. The ink in the middle is totally effaced with respect to that of the two outer edges. For the *verso*, the beginning of writing is completely effaced.
- Description: The ostraon is inscribed in black ink. The *recto* can be divided into two columns. The right one, column I, has 9 lines; the left one, column II, has only 8, its first line is totally effaced. The row division was probably meant by the scribe to convey that the workers were distributed onto two sides. The scribe seems to have been experienced in the art of writing as most of the inscription is fairly written. The ink of the bottom is slightly effaced with respect to that of the top. There are some handwriting errors committed by the scribe in column I. 5, and column II 3. 7. The *verso* is consisted only of 4 lines, and the beginning of it is completely lost.

[a.] "*Wn-nfr*" is identified here as the son of "*Pn-Ỉmn*" despite the fact that word "*s3*" is not yet preserved. "*Pn-Ỉmn*" is that workman whose lifetime span probably extended from year 3 of Amenmesse's reign down to year 15 of Ramses III's. He was probably identified to be the son of "*Ḫ*ʿ-*m-w3s.t*".[80] The both names occurred in some documents; for example O. Ashm 57. [81] Another occurrence for the same association of the two names can be found in O. Cairo CG 25556 and dated to year 5 of Seti II.[82] In these mentioned examples, "*Wn-nfr*" was not described as the son of "*Pn-Ỉmn*". However, the only vivid occurrence which attributes "*Wn-nfr*" explicitly as the son of "*Pn-Ỉmn*" is P. Berlin P 10496; this papyrus represents a quarrel between "*Wn-nfr*" with "*Ỉmn-m-ip.t*" as the former threw the mummy of the mistress of the latter out of the tomb. In this papyrus which is dated to year 21 of Ramses III, the parentage citation of the two names is direct enough (vso. 7).[83] At the end, this matter was settled by an oath. Then we learn from Davies that "*Pn-Ỉmn*" was evidently still alive until year 21 of Ramses III not to year 15. We might be able to go even further to state that this workman has appeared to be mentioned in year 24 of king Ramses III, in a legal dispute concerning the ownership of a tomb.[84]

[b.] "*Ỉmn-m-i(pt)*" is written incomplete but we can restore it in this manner. Having stated above the span of time to this ostracon, we can probably identify him as the workman whose lifetime span extended from the end of the XIXth Dynasty down to sometime of the reigning years of king Ramses IV. This hypothesis is based on the occurrences of his name along with "*Wn-nfr*" son of "*Pn-Ỉmn*". For example, his name appeared in O. Ashm 655 from the second half of Ramses III.[85] In addition, in O. DeM 236 which bears list of names and from year 1 of Ramses IV; "*Ỉmn-m-i(pt)*" (vso. I 4) is mentioned amongst a group of workmen along with "*Wn-nfr*" "rto. I, 2" who might have probably been "*Wn-nfr* son of *Pn-imn*".[86]

---

[80] Davies 1999, 5.6 (chart 2).

[81] This ostracon is dated to early-mid years of king Siptah by Collier 2004, 14-18, 154 (description, commentary, photograph).

[82] Collier 2004, 41-42, 156 (description, commentary).

[83] Lüddeckens 1994, vol. 4, 67, no. 92 (description; transcription and transliteration of recto 1 and verso 14).

[84] Davies 1999, 5-6.

[85] McDowell 1995, 32 (photograph, commentary).

[86] Helck 2002, 367 (translation in outline of content).

c "*Ḫ*ʿ*-m-ip.t*" might be the workman of the right side of the workforce whose name appeared in an undated ostracon (O. Gardiner 57).[87] Kitchen attributes it however to the XXth dynasty (the reign of Ramses III). Davies places this ostracon to the end of the XIXth dynasty.[88] I would rather agree with Kitchen's attribution as a result of the dating layout of the ostracon in question just drawn up above.
d "*Nḫt-Ỉmn*" might be identified with the workman of the same name who was married to the daughter of the "*M*ʿ*-ḫ3-ib*". The latter was the daughter of "*P3-šdw*", the soldier of the gang. It is known that "*P3-šdw*" started off his career during the reign of Seti I.[89] However, "*Nḫt-Ỉmn*" might have be the same person who was represented in TT 267 at Deir el-Medna. This tomb belongs to the official "*Ḥ3y*" who was the "*idn.w*" down to the year 31 of Ramses III's reign and contemporary to "*Nḫt-Ỉmn*".[90] In fact, that would be rather plausible as the latter was mentioned in P. Turin Cat. 1880 (rto IV 9); it is safely dated to year 29 of Ramses III.[91]
e. "*Ḫnmw-(nḫt)*" can probably be identified with the workman who appeared on a workmen list in an ostracon dated either to Ramses III or to Ramses V.[92] However, he never appeared with the individual "*Wn-nfr*" except in this ostracon.
f.. "*Ỉmn-ḫ*ʿ*w* son of *Ḥ3y*" could be probably identified with the workman of that name who is mentioned in O. Cairo CG 25804 (a list of names with quantities of wood and unspecified commodity (plaster?).[93] This ostracon is dated by kitchen to year 6 of Ramses IV. As a matter of fact, "*Ỉmn-ḫ*ʿ*w*" was never attributed as a son of "*Ḥ3y*", the foreman whose time span extended from year 3 of Merenptah to year 19 of Ramses III.[94] That makes the attribution very problematic as it is stated above that the post of "Foreman" was rather hereditary in the history of Deir el-Medina working community. Therefore, the son of a "foreman" was expected to be installed in his father's post.[95] Accordingly, we may be entitled to confirm the parentage of the foreman "*Ḥ3y*" to a son who occupied a post of workman. However, this is the first time we ever encounter such odd association. We can not rule out completely the possibility of encountering another "*Ḥ3y*" not the foreman.
g. "*P3-r*ʿ*-ḥtpw*" could be identified with that workman who appeared in O. DeM 556 in the XXth dynasty; this ostracon is dated by Kitchen to Ramses III.[96] In addition, he is mentioned in an ostracon "O. DeM 580" which holds a deposition account made by this workman against the Water-carrier "*Knr*". He also appeared in O. Michaelides 5 which dates to year 26 of Ramses III. Therefore, this ostracon helps us confirm that this workman was active in the last reigning years of king Ramses III. What is little enigmatic is that this is the first time he ever appears in other documents with some workmen like "*Wn-nfr*" son *Pn-Ỉmn*", "*Ỉmn-ḫ*ʿ*w* son *Ḥ3y*".
h. "*Mn-n3*" could be that workman who appeared together with "*P3-r*ʿ*-ḥtpw*" in an ostracon (O. DeM 10046) which bears a workmen list. This ostracon dates to Ramses III's reign.[97]
i. "*Sbk-ms*" could probably be that workman who appeared on a workman names' list (O. DeM 831) which dated to Ramses III's reign.[98] According to the personal names, Grandet suggests that "*Sbk-ms*" is the workman whose time span can be confined between year 31 of Ramses III and year 6 of Ramses IV. Thus we would be more inclined here to place the ostracon in question somewhere within these years.
j. "*Nb-imn.t(.t)*" is such rare name which appeared in very limited number of ostraca and received meagre consideration from scholars. Most of his name's occurrences can date to the XIXth dynasty.

---

87 KRI VII, 314 (transcription) rto. II:6.
88 Davies 1999, 249.
89 Černy 2004, 248.
90 Valbelle 1975, 19 and 29.
91 Ventura 1986, 90, 101, 121-123, 139 and 140 (transliteration and translation of recto I 1-6; recto II 6, 8-12, 15-16, 19-20; recto III 4-5, 7-15.
92 Helck 2002, 408-409 (translation).
93 KRI VI, 147-148 (transcriptions of present and earlier text).
94 Černy 2004, 125 (chart).
95 Ibid, 126.
96 KRI V, 592 (transcription).
97 Grandet 2006 51, 237 (photographs, facsimiles, transcriptions, description, transliteration, translation, commentary).
98 Grandet 2003, 1, 11, 197-199 (photographs, facsimile, description, transcription, transliteration, translation, commentary).

For example, O. BM EA 5634[99], O. DeM 60[100], O. DeM 286[101] and O. IFAO 371[102] have been placed by several scholars within the XIXth dynasty (specifically Ramses II's reign). That would render the ostracon in question very problematic in terms of the dating layout we have established at the beginning. However, in O. Louvre 13156 being dated to the XIXth (Ramses II), where there are mentioned the children names of "*Nb-imn.t(.t)*", there was mentioned another "*Nb-imn.t(.t)*" (line 1).[103] He was probably just a little child at the time of this ostracon. So we may assume that he could be another "*Nb-imn.t(.t)*" the son of a father with the same name. Accordingly, we can learn that "*Nb-imn.t(.t)*" is such individual who lived down into probably Ramses IV's reign.

k. "*P3-nḫt-ꜥ3*" could probably be that individual who appeared in P. Turin Cat. 54021 (rto I 9). This Papyrus is dated to year 10 of Ramses IX. [104] This individual appeared probably at the end of Ramses III and lived further, down into Ramses XI. This can be demonstrated by his appearance in (P. Turin. Cat. 1898 + P. Turin Cat. 1926 + P. Turin Cat.1937 + P. Turin Cat. 2094).[105]

l. "*Ḫnmw –ms(w)*" could be identified with that workman who appeared in O. Cairo CG 25553 (lines 2 and 4). This ostracon is dated to year 12 of Ramses III.[106]

m. "*Ḥwy-nfr*" could be identified with that individual who appeared in O. Michaelides 2 and P. Berlin P 10496 mentioned above.

n- For "*P3-ḥtpw*" or "*P3-rꜥ-ḥtpw*", I am wondering whether we can identify him with that individual of line 5 in the ostracon in question or not. In line 9 there is an added "*w*" which may have been just a marker to differentiate between the two names. Therefore, we would be more inclined to think that there were two different persons.

o- "*(dmḏ) s 15*" is such number which reminds us of that one of the right gang in year 64 of Ramses II's reign.[107] The same number has been attested in O. DeM 621 (completed by O. IFAO 1080), *recto*; the first two places on the list were allocated to the foreman and the scribe. We are wondering whether this organisation can be applied to the ostracon in question or not. If yes, the first two effaced names were destined for these two individuals. However, there remains a misleading point; the number attested does not correspond to the exact number of workmen written on this ostracon. We are wondering whether this can be considered as a handwriting error in estimating the number of the workmen, committed by the scribe. The problem is that there are three blank places caused by the effacement of the ink on the top of the ostracon in question. Therefore, we would not be able to estimate the number of workmen as there could have been repetition in names.

p- For "*P3-imi-r-iḥ.w*", despite the damage, he could be restored in this manner. He is the workman who appeared in KVO 1 and whose lifetime span could be confined between years 1 of Siptah to the middle of the XXth dynasty.

Schematic prosopography:

In dating KVO 5, one of the key persons on whom we may rely to confine our dating framework is "*P3-wr-ꜥ3*". As mentioned in the Edition of texts Chapter (KVO 5, column I, *recto* 7), his lifetime can be outlined down to year 10 of Ramses IX. The beginning of his working career was sometime at the end of Ramses III's reign.[108] His title was "the scribe of the right gang" whose father was "*Twt-m-ḥb*". It is really puzzling the fact that in this ostracon his name is not affiliated with any sort of administrative position. Therefore, we would be inclined to assign him to the labour class, rather than the scribal one. Then we may infer that there might have been two persons with the same name. Or we are encountering one workman who was promoted from the labour class to the scribal one. On the

[99] Grandet, 2002, 167, 315-317, no. 113 (photographs, description, translation, commentary, bibliography).
[100] Helck 1965, vol. V (845) (translation); KRI III, 563 (transcription).
[101] Černý 1939, 12, pl. 12 (description, transcription).
[102] Černy MSS, 103.20 (description, transcription).
[103] KRI III, 547-48.
[104] KRI VI, 633-636 (transcription of recto and verso II 1-5); Helck 2002,, 498, 499 and 501 (translation of recto I-III, IV 1-10, and verso II 1-4).
[105] Beckerath 1994, 29-33 (transcription and translation of verso dockets a and c; commentary).
[106] Allam 1973, 57-58, no. 28 (translation, commentary).
[107] Černy 2004, 105.
[108] Davies, 1999, 175.

other hand, we have learnt that the lifetime of "*P3-imi-r-iḥ.w*" had started off by year 1 of king Siptah and ended by the middle of the XXth dynasty. If we say that he commenced his career when he was 18 years old and lived until the middle of the XXth dynasty; that implies that he died around 1134 B.C, when he was around 68 years old which is very long lifetime. If so, it follows that KVO 5 probably falls between year 1 of Siptah and the first two years of Ramses VII.

Classification:
For KVO 5, the proper names of individuals are mentioned without any reference to a specific event. However the workmen's names divided onto two columns may be as a reference to the two gangs.[109] If we look at the ostraca of Deir el-Medina, which bear the same account nature, we will realise that there is no difference, to some extent, in the use of terminology; the setting is amost the same.[110]

---

[109] cft. O. DeM 212, O. DeM 236, and O. DeM 243.
[110] cft. O. DeM 209, O. DeM 339 and O. DeM 389, all absence accounts.

KVO 6 (Pl. VI; fig. 6)
O. Cairo JE 72467 (SR 1482)
A letter to a vizier

Transliteration

(1) [*<ḥḳꜣ> ꜥnḫ (.w) w)ḏꜣ(.w) s(nb.w)*]
(2) [*nb nrw*[a] *ꜥꜣ hnhn*[b]] *dr*[c] *ẖn*[d]
(3) [*dỉt tšỉ*[e] *n*[sic]*.f n mrwt.f*[f] *<Wsr-ḫprw-Rꜥ-mr-ỉmn> ꜥnḫ(.w) (w)ḏꜣ(.w) s(nb.w)*]
(4) [[*sꜣ Rꜥ*]*<stỉ-mr-n-ptḥ> ꜥnḫ(.w) (w)ḏꜣ(.w) s(nb.w)*]
(5) [*pꜣ bꜣkw n nb.f ṯꜣy-ḫw*[g] *ꜥnḫ(.w) (w)ḏꜣ(.w) s(nb.w) ḥr wnm.ỉ-nsw*][h]
(6) [*ỉmỉ-r nỉwt*[i] *ṯꜣtỉ Ḥrw*[j] *hꜣb pw rdỉ rḫ Pꜣy.ỉ*]
(7) [*nb ky (ḥr) swḏꜣ*[k] *ỉb n Pꜣy.ỉ nb r-nty*[l] *tꜣ st*]
(8) [*n ꜥꜣ*[m] *ꜥnḫ(.w) (w)ḏꜣ(.w) s(nb.w) pꜣy.(ỉ) nb ꜥnḫ(.w) (w)ḏꜣ(.w) s(nb.w) dbḥ (?)* ti[n]]
(9) [*nsw ??r ỉkr*]

Translation

(1) To [the ruler], "L. P. H", to....
(2) [The Lord of Terror the great of jubilation], the separator of rebel,
(3) [(the Lord) causing him (the rebel) to flee and to love [*Wsr-ḫprw-Rꜥ-mr-ỉmn*] "L. P. H"],
(4) [son of the god "*Rꜥ*", [Seti (II) Merenptah] "L. P. H"],
(5) [the humble servant of his "Lord", the Fan-bearer "L. P. H" on the right hand of the king, the governor of Thebes],
(6) [the vizier "*Ḥrw*". It is to send and to give my "Lord" to know (that)],
(7) [another (thing) is going to make sound the heart of my "Lord" in respect to the tomb of (the)]
(8) [pharaoh "L. P. H", my Lord "L. P. H", (it) is in need of] ....
(9) a royal (?) (?) to be excellent.

Commentary

- Dimension: 13 x 19.5 cm
- Material: Limestone
- Provenance: Valley of the Kings (Davis'excavations).
- Publication: Darresy 1927, 174: the ostracon was published (transcription- little commentary); Černy MSS 106-15 (only transcription and little information about the year of excavations of Davis 1905-06).
- Dating: Since the name of king Seti II is mentioned on this ostracon, we can safely date it to the Late XIXth Dynasty (1214-1204 B.C).[111]Unfortunately, the exact year of this event is not recorded.
- Condition: The ostracon is large slab; however the right and the upper sides are partially chipped off and so are the edges. The writing is fully effaced and only on the upper-left side there are some of damaged signs. However, it was easily to be restored by the scholars in the past. Daressy had mentions that it was found in Biban el-Molouk in the excavations conducted by Th. Davis and there was designated a mark "X 2". The ink is completely gone except little traces spread in some parts over the ostracon; the right side has still some traces of writings as well as line 2 on the upper left side.
- Description: The ostracon seems to have been written in black ink as for the residues left from the original writing. It is inscribed only on one side and has been written in 8 lines; almost complete and nothing missing except in some parts (line 1 upper left-side). There is under the line 8 some writing which represents the signature of who wrote this letter. By virtue of

---

[111] Baines & Malek 1980, 37.

Daressy and Černy's endeavour, we could be working now on their transcription and attempting to add further information about the philological structure of some phrases. From the residues of writing, we can infer how fair the handwriting was.

[a.] "*nb nrw*" or the "the king of Terror" is rather an epithet which refers to the king himself. the word "*nrw*" has usually two determinatives; one is the vulture head with either the standing leaning man, holding a stick [112]or the forearm holding a stick (KRI 5, 11, 129). In both cases, it was translated as "terror or awe". The combination between "*nb*" and "*nrw*" [Wb 2, 278.8; LGG III, 664 ff] is merely a possessive construction which conveys ownership.[113] This combination has appeared in a range of documents as an epithet referring to the king.[114]

[b.] "*hnhn*" means jubilation (Wb 2, 496.1). "*ʿꜣ hnhn*" is a "*nfr ḥr*" construction which means great of jubilation. The adjectival phrase expresses ownership and the adjectival quality is referred to the owner (the king).[115]

[c.] "*dr*" means dispel (Lesko IV, 138.3); in P. Leiden I, 348, 4R7. In this papyrus, it was translated rather as a verb. However, the infinitive form of the verb is used to refer to the doer of the action that is the king.

[d.] "*ḫn*" means rebel (Wb 3, 288, 17-18: FCD 191). The "" and ", yod" have probably been added to the stem form of this word as a result of some spoken language influences.[116] In fact, the hieratic texts are rich of using such final phonetics.[117]

[e.] "*tši*" means to flee in (Lesko IV, 98).[118] It is preceded by a causative verb "*dit*" which certainly renders the whole sentence as a causative structure (*dit +sdm.f* form, subjunctive).[119] The subject of the infinitive form "*tši*" is preceded by an "*n*"; this preposition seems to be odd before the suffix.

[f.] "*mrwt.f*" means "to love" (Lesko I, 226).[120]We would rather consider this "*sḏm.f*" as another subjunctive form which is governed by the same causative verb "*dit*". The contrast in meaning between the two words "*tši*" "*mrwt*" may probably highlight the paramount power of the king. In other words, the vizier probably wanted to assert the power of the king by mentioning his capability of deserting a rebel and at the same time he probably wanted to hide the hatred which may arise from the rebel against the king by stating word "love": despite the fact that the king could desert a rebel, the rebel still loves the king as the ideal image of the king should be highly presented.

[g.] "*ṯꜣy-ḫw*" it is attested in the Temple of Amun at Karnak, Hypostyle hall, north wall, in the register which depicts the warfare against the Libyans.[121] It is a title which was held by high ranking functionaries around the Pharaoh; an example for that can be found in the letter on the preparations for the Opet Festival in O. Gradiner 362.[122] In this letter, the scribe Ramose greets his superior (master), the royal scribe and the superintendent of cattle, "Hati". Furthermore, the same title has occurred in O. DeM 1248 and O. Bruxelles E. 6444 which both bear the teachings of Amenmhat.[123]

[h.] "*ḥr wnm.i-nsw*" means on the right hand of the kings (LÄ VI, 1162; vgl. Wb 5, 348.4 and 1, 322.6-7; vgl. Lesko, IV, 104). The same title has appeared in O. DeM 114.[124]

[i.] (*imi-r niwt*) is another title which indicated to the governor of the city that is Thebes.[125] It was mentioned in the tomb of the Vizier, Paser, no. 106.[126] It is transcribed:

---

[112] Gardiner 1911, 1, 5, 5.

[113] Allen 2000, 63.

[114] Lapp 1997, pl. 2-9. This papyrus comes from Thebes and can date from Hatchepsut to Amenophis II and is written in cursive hieroglyphic; Goyon 1972 II, 5; Verhoeven 2001, 308-318.

[115] Allen 2000, 64.

[116] Peust 1999, 137, §3.13.1 and §3.13.2.

[117] Grandet 2003, *passim*.

[118] The same word has been used with same meaning in, Peet 1930, Amherst (pl. 15) 4.2.

[119] Allen 2000, 254; Johnson1986, tables in P. 82: this page stresses on the historical development of the Egyptian verbal System.

[120] Erichsen 1933, 1, 22, 10.

[121] KRI I, 20-234, VII, 425; RITA I, 17-19; RITANC I, 23-24.

[122]Černy & Gardiner 1957, 29, pl. CVII; KRI III, 637, and KRI Translation III, 435 f..; Wente 1990, 119 f.

[123] Posener 1955, 61-72; Posener 1951-1972, 37-38 and pl. 62-62a; Dorn 2004, 38-55.

[124] Černy 1935a, pl. 1-1A; KRI III, 45-46 and KRI Translation III, 31 ff.; Allam 1973, 91-2, no. 59.

[hieroglyphs] and can transliterate as follows: *t3y-ḫw* (*G7*[sic]) *ʿnḫ* (*.w*) (*w*)*ḏ3*(*.w*) *s*(*nb.w*) *ḥr wnm.i-nsw*. This title was originated in the New Kingdom and has no any previous background in the preceding periods.

j. "*Ḥrw*" is the vizier who lived during the successive reigns of Seti II, Siptah, Setnakhte and Ramses III. His name has been mentioned on a very wide range of monuments among which there are also several ostraca.[127]

k. "*swḏ3 ib*" is an expression often used as an infinitival phrase in letters; it is one of the idioms which are characteristic of letter typology.[128]

l. "*r-nty*" means "quote" (Lesko, Dictionary II, 50). It has been frequently mentioned in several letters; again it means "with respect to".[129]

m. [hieroglyphs] is an expression which refers to an area of some extent.[130]It is another topographical term which conveys undetermined area in the Theban necropolis during the ruling king as *pr-ʿ3*, in that time; it was designated only to refer to the living king.[131] Černy gave also a reference to an unpublished ostracon kept in the Metropolitan Museum on which there is this inscription [hieroglyphs] (14.6.27). This may imply that this term was used rather when the king was still alive. In some occurrences of the same term, it was mentioned that "*st pr-ʿ3*" has five walls.[132] Therefore, this designation might mean the tomb of the pharaoh. This hint would be the most plausible one to rely on.

n. "*dbḥ*" means "in need of" (Wb 5, 439.6-440.1).[133] The verb could be classified as Pseudo-participle as the ending "*ti*" is added to the stem of the verb. Such kind of verbs describes an accomplished result of a previous action or the state of something/someone.[134] The structure of this form is very often (subject + Pseudo-Participle). In the ostracon in question, the subject could be logically defined as the "tomb". The whole construction is rather descriptive in meaning. The scribe wanted to convey that "the tomb is need of something...".

Such type of non-literary documents reflects rather the spoken language of the Ancient Egyptians. "It is just a quick substitution to the spoken communication as well as that of today". [135] It belongs to diverse classes of the society, ranging from kings, passing over with the private officials and ending up with ordinary people. The letters could be addressed from kings to the Egyptians directly or the contrary.[136] There are some infinitival phrases which were commonly used in letters, like the causative form [hieroglyphs] "make the heart sound"; other epistolary formulae like *iḫ rḫ=k - m ʿnḫ wḏ3 snb* (*m ḥs.w.t ...*) *- NN* (*ḥr nḏ ḫr.t*/*swḏ3 ib*) *n NN - nfr snb=k - r nty - h3b pw r rdi.t rḫ - ḥnʿ ḏd - ky swḏ3 ib - ky ḏd*.[137]It used to have such account either in the Valley of the Kings[138] or in Deir el-Medina.[139] Looking over the two outcomes of these two sites, we can infer that there is no much difference between the letters of Deir el-Medina and those of the Valley of the Kings in terms of setting. Unsurprisingly, the two letter outcomes had been written by the same persons, handling almost the same quotidian needs. As a matter of fact the bulk of the letters comes from Western Thebes where there was based a small group of administrators originally associated with the royal Necropolis.[140]

---

125 Al-Ayedi 2006 , 74.

126 PM[2] I:1, 219-24; KRI I, 285 ff; KRI III, 1 ff.

127 Pomorska 1987, 188-191. The scholar has collected all the citations on which the name of this vizier occurs.

128 Allen 2000, 387.

129 Černy 1939, Bruxelles, 2R4, 17R6.

130 Černy 2004, 70- 72.

131 Černy 1929, 248, pl. XL.III (R° 7).

132 RAD 49, 15; 52, 14.

133 Brovarski 2001, 38, 108-110; text fig. 4; pl. 75-80a; fig. 17, 21-23, text-fig. 4; vgl. Urk I 65.15-66.14.

134 Neveu 1998, 52-55.

135 Wente 1967, *passim*.

136 Allen 2000, 386.

137 Ibid, 387.

138 O. Cairo CG 25561 ; O. Cairo CG 25644.

139 O. DeM 228; O. DeM 246; O. DeM 248.

140 Sweeny 2001, 11.

KVO 7 (Pl. VII; fig. 7a, b)
O. Cairo JE 72468 (SR 1483)
A list of workmen present

Transliteration

(*recto* a)

(1) [*iw Kꜣ*] *sꜣ Rʿ-*(*ms*)[b]
(2)[*iw*] *Ḥrw-m-wiꜣ*
(3) *iw Pꜣ-ym.w*[e]
(4) *iw Ỉmn-m-ipt*[g]
(5) [*iw*] [*H̱nmw-msw*][i]
(6) [*iw*] [...]

[*iw*] *Ḥrw-m-wiꜣ*[a] (1)
iw Pꜣ-šdw[c] (2)
[*iw*] *Nb-nḫt.w*[d] (3)
iw ʿꜣ-nḫt.w[f] (4)
Ỉw ʿꜣ-phty[h] (5)
iw Kꜣ-sꜣ[j] (6)
[...](7)

(*recto* b)

iw[*Nb-nfr*[k] *sꜣ Wꜣd-ms*] (1)
iw Rʿw-wbn[l] (2)

Translation

(*recto* a)

(1) [*Kꜣ*] *sꜣ Rʿ* [has come]
(2) *Ḥrw-m-wiꜣ* [has come]
(3) *Pꜣ-ymw* has come
(4) *Ỉmn-m-ipt* has come
(5) [*H̱nmw-m*]*sw* [has come]
(6) [...] [has come]

M-wiꜣ [has come] (1)
Pꜣ-šdw has come (2)
Nb-nḫt.w [has come] (3)
ʿꜣ-nḫt-tw has come (4)
ʿꜣ-pḥty has come (5)
Kꜣ-sꜣ has come (6)
[...](7)

(*recto* b)

[*Nb-nfr sꜣ Wꜣd-ms* has come](1)
Rʿw-wbn has come (2)

Transliteration

(*verso* a)

	(1) *iw* (*?*)	
	(2) *iw Ḳꜣ-ḥ*[*ꜣ*][n]	*iw Ỉmn-*(*?*) (1)
5	(3) *iw Ḫʿ-m-nwn*[p]	*iw Ḥwy*[m] *sꜣ Ḥwy-nfr* (2)
5 8	(4) *iw Mʿ-k* (*y*)*-rmṯ-tw.f*	
5		
5 8 (*?*)	(5) *P*[*tḥ*]*-šdw*	*iw Rw-tḥ*[o] (3)
(*5*) *8*	(6) (?) *Ḥtpw*	*Ḥsi-sw-nb.f* (4)
5	(7) [*Ḫꜣ*]*mw*	*iw Ḥwy sꜣ Ḫʿw*[q](5)
5 8	(8) [*Pꜣ*]*-imy-r-iḥ.w*	(*?*) *sꜣ Pn-nbw* (6)
5	(9) [...]	

(*verso* b)

9 *219*
16

4

Translation

(*verso* a)

	(1) (?) has come	*Ỉmn*-(?) has come (1)
	(2) *Ḳꜣ-ḥꜣ* has come	*Ḥwy* son of *Ḥwy-nfr* has come(2)
	(3) *Ḫꜥ-m-nw* has come	
5		
5 8	(4) *Mꜥ-k* (*y*) *rmṯ-tw.f* has come	*Rw-tḫ* has come (3)
5		*Ḥsi-sw-nb.f* has come (4)
5 8	(5) *P*[*tḥ*]-*šdw*	*Ḥwy* son of *Ḫꜥw* has come (5)
(5) 8	(6) *Ḥtpw*	(?) son of *Pn-nbw* (has come) (6)
5 8		
5	(7) *Ḫꜣmw*	
5 8	(8) *Pꜣ-mr-kꜣ*	
5	(9) [...]	

(*verso* b)

9 219

16

4

Commentary

- Dimension: a, 6.5 x 12 cm, b, 3 x 6 cm
- Material : Limestone
- Provenance: Valley of the Kings (Davis'excavations).
- Cft. Černy MSS 106-16 and 106-16f.[141]
- Dating: According to the Special Register, the ostracon can date to the end of the XIXth dynasty.
- Condition: The ostracon is composed of four glued fragments; one of them does not join. It seems that there are other fragments missing; the most significant missing piece is that one at the bottom. The ink of the right part of the "*recto* a" is in good condition in respect with that of the left one. The ink of "*recto* b" is also in a good state. The ink of the "*verso* a, b" is significantly legible. However, almost in the middle of this side the writing is slightly effacing. The fractures between the fragments can cause somewhat hardship in reading.
- Description: The ostracon is inscribed on two sides in black ink. The "*recto* a" is composed of two columns. Column "I" has 7 written lines; while column II has only 6 lines inscribed. The last line of column I is completely effaced. The writing of column I is more preserved than that of column II. For "*recto* b", it has two inscribed lines. Line "1" is completely lost from at the beginning; however the rest of the line is still preserved. With regard to the "*verso*", it is composed of three columns. Column "I" has only 6 lines; while column "II" has the longest inscribed part "9 lines". The third column "III" has only numbers which may correspond to some rations not specified. It might have been as long as column II but its upper part is completely lost with the breakage. However, the writing is running down until the same level of column II. For "*verso* b", it might be consisted of two lines with higher numbers. It is hard to reconstruct what they refer to.

The names taking place in this ostracon are mentioned without any specification of a particular job. Therefore, we may be able to say that it is a list of workmen. What is distinct about it is that the

[141] Collier 2004, 48-50, 157 (description, commentary).

"*recto*" is composed of two columns which may signify that there might have been two gangs; the right and left ones.

[a.] "*Ḥrw-m-wiꜣ*" might be that workman who was mentioned on O. Ashm 57 which could date to year 2 of Siptah's reign.[142] He was mentioned also on O. Cairo CG 25519 which can date to year 1 of king Siptah.[143] In fact, most of his name's citations are dated to the end of the XIXth dynasty (Amenmesse and Siptah).[144] Why the name of "*Ḥrw-m-wiꜣ*" has appeared twice, one time on the right gang column I, 1 and the other one on the left one column II, 2? The answer would be that it could have been a mistake committed by the scribe; or the two names might have probably referred to two different persons.

[b.] "[*Kꜣ*] *sꜣ Rꜥ-*(*ms*)" is that workman who lived in the second half of the XIXth dynasty.[145] The name is missing the first part. He was mentioned with the just abovementioned workman in O. Cairo CG 25523 which dates to year 2 of king Siptah.[146] He was also mentioned in O. Cairo CG 25779 which dates to year 1 of Amenmesse.[147]Furthermore, his name happened to be written in O. DeM 912 which dates to year 1 or 2 of king Siptah.[148]

[c.] "*Pꜣ-šdw*" can be identified with that workman who appeared in O. Cairo CG 25517 which can date to year 6 of king Seti II.[149] However Collier dates it to year 1 of king Siptah.[150] At any rate, this is the span of time to which this ostracon can assign.

[d.] "*Nb-nḫt.w*" could be that workman who is mentioned in O. Cairo Carnarvon 343 which can date to the reign of Amenmesse.[151] He can also be found in O. Varille 22 which can date to either Seti II or Siptah.[152]

[e.] For "*Pꜣ-ym.w*", he can be identified with that workman who appeared in O. Cairo CG 25781 which can date to Siptah's reign.[153]

[f.] "*ꜥꜣ-nḫt.w*" can be identified with that workman who appeared in (Černy graffiti, p. 26, pl. 71) as the father of the scribe "*Wn-nfr*". He moved between the right and left sides of the gang.[154]

[g.] "*Imn-m-ipt*" can be that workman who is mentioned on the O. Ashm 57 which has a list of names and is dated to the year 2 of Siptah's reign.

[h.] "*ꜥꜣ-pḥty*" can be the workman who appeared in O. Ashm 232 which dates to late Seti II-early Siptah.[155]

[i.] "[*Ḫnmw-msw*]" could be that workman who appeared in O. Cairo CG 25797 which can date after year 5 of Siptah's reign.[156]

[j.] For "*Kꜣ-sꜣ*", by the second half of the XIXth dynasty, there appeared two workmen who bore the same name. One of them is the son of "*Rꜥ-ms*" (see "[b]") and the second might have been the son of "*Pꜣ-nb*".[157]However, there appeared another workman with the same name who had together with "*Kꜣ* son of *Rꜥ-ms*" got involved in crimes committed by the foreman.[158] There have might been many workmen with the same name, working together by the end of the XIXth dynasty and the beginning of the XXth dynasty.

---

[142] Helck 2002 , 172-173 (translation).

[143] Collier 2004, 35-36, 155 (description, commentary).

[144] Look it up in O. Turin 57388 published in, López 1978-1984, vol. III, 29 (description), pl. 125-125a (facsimile and transcription of verso.

[145] Davies 1999, 273-274.

[146] Černy 1935b, 11-12 (description, transcription of erased text), 26* (transcription), pl. XVIII (facsimile); KRI IV, 329-330.

[147] KRI IV, 211-216.

[148] Grandet 2004, xvii, 4, 88-89, 340-343 (photographs, facsimile, transcription, description, transliteration, translation, commentary).

[149] Wimmer, 1995, vol. I, 48-50 (transcription of delta ; but see Wimmer 1995, vol. I, 22).

[150] Collier 2004, 25-27, 34-35, 155 (description, commentary).

[151] KRI VII , 244 (transcription).

[152] Černý MSS, 43.34 (description and transcription).

[153] Helck 2002, 194 (translation).

[154] Collier 2004, 1-13, 130, 146.

[155] Helck, 2002, 113 (outline of content).

[156] Collier 2004, 58, 61-64, 157 (description, commentary).

[157] Bierbrier 1982, 129.

[158] Černy 1929, P. Salt 124, rto. 2:10.

k. "*Nb-nfr* son of *W3d-ms*" is one of grandsons of the foreman "*Nb-nfr*". We know that "*W3ḏ-ms*" career can be firmly attributed to the first half of Ramses II's reign. By his marriage to one of the daughters of the foreman whose name is mentioned above, he got his affiliation to this family.[159] "*Nb-nfr*" however could be that workman who appeared by the end of the XIXth dynasty.
l. "*Rˁ-wbn*" can be that workman who appeared in O. Cairo CG 25513 which dates to Siptah-Tausert.[160] Another occurrence of the same name can be found in O. Medelhavsmuseet MM 14126 which can date to the end of the XIXth dynasty.[161]
m. "*Ḥwy* son of *Ḥwy-nfr*" can be identified with the workman who appeared in O. Černy 7 which is dated to the reign of Amenmesse.[162]
n "*Ḳ3-ḫ3*" could probably be that workman who lived during the latter half of the XIXth dynasty.[163] His first appearance was in year 3 of Amenmesse.[164] He pursued his lifetime as a workman down to year 11 of king Ramses III.[165]
o. "*Rw-tḫ*" can be that workman who appeared towards the end of the XIXth dynasty. His name was always mentioned as a member of the left-side gang.[166] He happened to be punished severely, being beaten, as a result of a drunken behaviour.[167] His name did not come up until year 13 of Ramses III.[168]
p. "*Ḫˁ-m-nwn*" can be identified with the workman who appeared by the closing years of the XIXth dynasty.[169]
q. "*Ḫˁw*" is the owner of TT 214 in which there was depicted some of his family members. Amongst those represented, there was also "*Ḥwy*". We know that the latter's father lived in the second half of Ramses II's reign. However the son might have probably lived by the closing years of XIXth dynasty.

Schematic prosopography:
Among the high number of workmen's names on KVO 7, we would like to focus on the key persons that may be used as a vivid clue for dating. Once more, it comes to dealing with "*Ḥsi-sw-nb.f*" who has been systemically studied by Janssen.[170] He has stated that this workman progressed to the rank of "deputy" by year 14 of king Ramses III. Davies says that he had been a member of the left gang in Siptah's reign, following his transfer from the right one;[171] this hypothesis was first originated by Černy.[172] That can help us set out a dating framework for the ostracon in question to sometime within Siptah's reign, as in this ostracon, the person is assigned to the right gang not to the left one. With the appearance of the workman "*P3-imi-r-iḫ.w*" in this ostracon, we are constrained to count from year 1 of Siptah's reign for his first appearance in the records of the workcrew. In O. Cairo CG 25521 from year 1 and 2 of Siptah's reign, "*Ḥsi-sw-nb.f*" was mentioned among the workmen of the left gang. That implies that up to year 2 of Siptah, he had not yet been assigned to the right gang. Another workman "*Nb-nfr* son of *W3ḏ-ms*" can date from year 3 of king Amenmesse to year 2 of king Siptah.[173] On the basis of all this data, we may infer a more plausible date to this ostracon; either by the end of year 2 of king Siptah or at latest, by the beginning of year 3 of the same king.

Philiological aspect:

---

[159] Davies 1999, 217-218.
[160] KRI IV 433 (transcription).
[161] McDowell 1999, 62-63 no. 33 (translation).
[162] KRI VII, 243 (transcription).
[163] Davies 1999, 20.
[164] O. Cairo CG 25780, 8.
[165] O. Geneva MAH 12550, rto 3-4.
[166] Davies 1999, 245.
[167] O. Gardiner 37, rto. x^+1, x^+2.
[168] O. IFAO 1285, 2.
[169] Davies 1999, 251.
[170] Janssen 1982, 113
[171] Davies 1999, 33.
[172] Černy 2004, 304.
[173] Davies 1999, 235.

In some ostraca like KVO 7 which concern the presence of some workmen on certain days (sometimes no mention for any specific days), the scribe used to write "*iw*" with meaning "has come". This use of the qualitative is very common in the terminology of such accounts either in Deir el-Medina or the in the Valley of the Kings. In such structure, usually the verb should come in the second postion after the subject. However, here it stands at the beginning of the sentence to stress probably on the fisrt part "present" which is the main issue.[174]

[174] Neveu 1998, 80; P. Turin 2021. 2 8-9 in KRI VI, 740, 1-2.

KVO 8 (Pl. VIII; fig. 8a, b)
O. Cairo 72469 (SR 1484)
A list of workmen absent

Transliteration (*recto*)

1- [...] *(?) mw*[a] *n p3y.f šnn.t*[b]
2- [...] *3ḫ.t nfr.yt*[c] *r 3bd 2 3ḫ.t sw 18 iw.f mr*[d]
3- [...] *[Ḳ]n*[e] *Mry-rʿ*[f] *wsf 3bd 2 3ḫ.t* [...]
4- [...] *[3bd (?)] 3ḫ.t sw22 Ḳn Mry-r ʿ* [...]
5- [...]*Ḫ3mw*[g] *Ḳn Mry-rʿ* [...] [...]
6- *[Ḥrw] m-Wi3*[h] *Nb-imn*[i] *wsf* [...]
7- [...] *wsf.w 3bd 13ḫ.t* [...]
8- *[P3]-šdw*[j] *s3 Ḥḥ*([...]
9- [...]*s3 Ḥḥ Nb-smn Nb-nḫt[w]*

Translation *(recto)*

1- [...] (?) who is present and absent for his illness[...]
2- [...] (of) the inundation season until the second month of akhet, he was ill on day 18.
3- [...] *[Ḳ]n* and *Mry- rʿ* were absent the second month of akhet[...]
4- [...] [month (?)] of akhet, day 22, *Ḳn* and *Mry-rʿ* [...]
5- [...] *Ḫ3mw* and *Qn* and *Mry-rʿ* [...]
6- *[Ḥrw] m-wi3* and *Nb-imn* are absent [...]
7- [...] absentees, the first month of akhet [...]
8- *[P3]šdw* son of *Ḥḥ-nḫw*, and *Nb-smn* [...
9- [...] son of *Ḥḥ*, *Nb-smn* and *Nb-nḫt[w]*

Transliteration (*verso*)

(1) [...] *[Nḫw]-m-mwt*[k] *Ipwy*[l] *N3-[ḫy]*[m] *s3 Bw-ḳn (?)* [...]
(2) [...] *[N3]-ḫy s3 Bw-ḳn-tw.f I[pwy] (?)* [...]
(3) [...] *(?) sw 28 N3-ḫy [s3 Bw-ḳn tw-*[…] *Ḥwy*[n] *s3 Ḫʿ](w)* [...]
(4) [...] *[tw.f] Nḫw-m-mwt Pn-dw3ww*[o] *Ip (wy)* [...]
(5) [...] *Ḥ3y*[p] *wsf 3bd 3 3ḫt sw 3 ʿ3 n is.t* [...]
(6) [...] *[s3]-w3ḏyt*[q] *Pn-dw3ww Ipwy sš ḳd.w nfr*[r] [...]
(7) [...] *[s3] [w3ḏ]yt Ḥwy s3 Ḫʿw Ipwy wsf* [...]
(8) *[ws]f ʿ3 n is.t* [...]
(9) *(?)* [...]

Translation *(verso)*

(1) [...] *[Nḫw]-m-mwt, Ipwy,* and *N3-[ḫy]* son of *Bw-ḳn (?)* [...
(2) […] *[N3]-ḫy* son of *Bw-ḳn-tw.f,* and *I[pwy]* (?) […]
(3) […] (?) on day *28 N3-ḫy* [son of *Bw-ḳn tw-(.f),* and *Ḥwy* son of *Ḫʿ](w)*[…
(4) […] *[tw.f] Nḫw-m-mwt, Pn-dw3ww,* and *Ip (wy)*[…]
(5) […] *Ḥ3y* is absent, the Third month of the inundation season, on day 3, the chief of the gang […
(6) […]*W3ḏyt, Pn-dw3ww Ipwy,* the draftsman, and *(Ḥtp)-nfr*[…
(7) […] *[W3ḏ]yt Ḥwy* son of *Ḫʿw Ipwy* absent[…
(8) [...] [absent], the chief of the gang [...
(9) (?) [...]

Commentary

- Dimension: 12 x 11 cm
- Material: Limestone
- Provenance: Valley of the Kings (Davis'excavations)
- Cft. MSS Černy 106.19.
- Dating: According to the Special Register, the ostracon can date to XIX-XXth dynasty.
- Condition: The ink of the two sides is well preserved. There are some fractures which may render the reading in some points somehow difficult. The writing of the *recto* is more preserved in comparison to that of the *verso*.
- Description: This ostracon is broken into three fragments. It is obvious that the lines are incomplete; the right side has also some lost parts. The *recto* has 9 inscribed lines as well as the *verso*. Although the ostracon had been reassembled of three fragments which may cause some difficulty in reading some words in the middle, the black ink is still in good state. The *recto*'s writing is slightly more preserved than the *verso*'s. In general, what helps distinctly ensure precise decipherment is the repetition of certain words like *wsf* "deedless", (Wb1, 357.14), along with some proper names.We have found two small pieces being associated in the Special Register with this ostracon, designated (a, b). After examining their content which contains only numbers, we can assure that the two pieces are completely irrelevant. Therefore, we have decided to exclude them here. Therefore, we have decided to exclude them here and publish only the text of the bigger slabs.

(a) We may assume to read it as *wn* "who is present" and *nn* "who is absent". They have been cited deliberately by the scribe to address the content of this document. Since the content could be classified as "journal work calendar" recording absence of artisans, then both *wn* and *nn* would fit best in this content. However, there remains the additional enigmatic sign "*n*" which is quite irrelevant. On the other hand, there is some lost part before mentioning word *mw*. So we may assume that there could have been the infinitive form of verb "bring"; that is "*in.t*". If so, the phrase might be translated "those who bring water" or simply "bringing water". Then, the designation with the use of "*mw*" and "*šnn*" addresses the following content which concerns some absent workmen on certain days for bringing water or being ill.

(b) For *šnn* (Wb4, 515. 3-9), the first sign is the cord, read as *šnn.t*.[175] It fits best here in this context as the whole list concerns "journal work, list of absent personnel". However, the possessive pronoun *p3y.f* is masculine and *šnn.t* is feminine. Therefore, we may regard that as it was merely a handwriting mistake committed by the scribe. There is another possibility of reading the same sign which could be "*sn*". If so, that will make no sense in the context we are handling here.

(c) "*nfr.yt-r*" means "end" in (Wb2, 262.13-16; FCD 132), is defined as compound preposition.[176] McDowell has translated it as "first" in meaning when it refers to a longer span of time.[177] I think that it should be also translated as "first" in meaning here in this context. Then, the whole meaning would be "from the first of Akhet until month 2 of the same season".

(d) *iw.f mr* is typical administrative terminology. It has occurred in a considerable range of ostraca. For instance, in O. Ashm 37 (obv.7) [178], O. Cairo CG 51514 (rev 20, 22)[179], O. DeM 209 (obv. 14, rev. 17).[180]. The construction *iw.f mr* is circumstantial clause which

---

[175] Möller 1927, 47.

[176] Collier & Quirke 2004, pUC 32126, and the teaching of Kheti on O. DeM 1013 (rto.10).

[177] McDowell 1993, O. Glasgow D. 1925. 71 vso. 2, Pl. IXa. Here in this Ostracon, the reference of *nfr.t* is associated with *rnp.t*.

[178] Collier 2004, 78-79, 154 (description, commentary, photograph).

[179] Helck 2002, 140, 166-167 (outline of part of content).

[180] KRI IV, 217-219.

expresses an action in progress. Usually *iw* refers to an independent clause and has no value of time. In late Egyptian and Coptic, it is rather used as the mark of a clause of time or circumstance.[181] So here in this ostracon, we should translate the whole clause as "he was ill" which has the value of past continuous tense (imperfect). *iw.f mr* = *iw* + suffix + old perfective (stative or old perfective).

(e) *Ḳn*[182], he was probably the son of "*Bw-ḳn-tw.f*" who held the same title *sḏm-ꜥš m st-mꜢꜥt* "servant in the Place of Truth" and lived down to the first year of Ramses V.[183]

(f) For "*Mry-rꜥ*" or "*Rꜥ-mry*"[184], he could be identified with the "workman" of O. DeM 357 which could be dated to Ramses VI.[185] In this ostracon, he could probably be the "workman" quoted in O. DeM 357 whose time span extended down to Ramses VI's reign.

(g) "*ḪꜢm(w)*"[186], "workman", appeared in around 57 documents (for example O. Ashm 37, P. DeM 32. His time span, according to written sources, could be traced through from the reigns of Amenmesse, Seti II, and end of Siptah's reigns. A certain "*ḪꜢmy*" has appeared in year in year 26 or 36 of Ramses II's reign.[187] Many scholars have thought that there was only one "*ḪꜢmy*" who appeared from that year of Ramses II and lived down somewhere within the reigning years of king Siptah.[188] It is very puzzling to make a decisive distinction for this name but we would like to mention the attestations of his name in O. Turin N. 57082 together with *Ḥwy*, Son of *Ḥwy-nfr* ; [...], Son of [...]-*WꜢḏyt*, *KꜢsꜢ*, *ḪꜢm*, *Ḥrw-m-wiꜢ*, and *PꜢ-šdw*. It is noteworthy stating that both *Ḥrw-m-wiꜢ* and *ḪꜢmw* appeared together in several ostraca.

(h) [...]-*m-wiꜢ*[189], we propose to read this name as *Ḥrw-m-wiꜢ* a quarry workman, listed in P. Salt 124 (London, British Museum, BM 10055) among sixteen other workmen who were quarrying the king's tomb in Valley of the Kings. He could be assigned to the late XIXth dynasty, most probably the reign of Amenmesse.[190]

(i) Interesting enough is *Nb-smn*'s name which appeared in the same list of P. Salt 124. For *Nb-imn*[191], he held the title "the child of the tomb".[192] This title refers rather to the small job or occasional jobs assigned to those people who held it. It is known that he witnessed with a door-keeper to an oath when a donkey was being handed over (O.DeM 133; it dates to the first half of XXth dynasty) and testified later on this.

(j) This name could be restored as "*PꜢ-šdw*". In this ostracon, he is assigned to be the son of the workman "*Ḥh-nḫw*" who lived down to the end of the XIXth dynasty.

(k) *Nḫw-m-mwt* could probably be identified with the workman who was born, according to Bierbrier's calculation, in year 25th of Ramses II's reign.[193] He escalated in his working career until he occupied the post of foreman between years 11 and 15 of Ramses III's reign; by that time he was very elderly man.[194] However, until the time of the ostracon in question, he could have probably still been an ordinary workman. On the other hand, his name's citation at the beginning of the *verso*'s side throws some doubt on his current position during the time of this ostracon. The fact that his name is not followed by any

---

[181] Bakir 1983, 41,§124.
[182] RPN I, 334.
[183] Davies 1999, 221, §65; for topographical designations, see Adrom 2008, 12-14.
[184] RPN II , 160.
[185] Ibid, 353 footnote 5.
[186] RPN I, 262.
[187] López 1978-194, 42, pl. 49/49a.
[188] Demarée 1983, 104; KRI III, 530.
[189] Ibid, 247.
[190] Davies 1999, 12.
[191] Ibid, 186.
[192] Bogoslovsky 1981, 5-21.
[193] Bierbrier 1982, 201.
[194] Davies 1999, 47.

affiliation makes us very sceptic regarding assigning any specific position other than a normal workman.

(l) The setting framework of this ostracon might direct us to attribute it to the end of the XIXth dynasty. However, "*Ỉpwy*" was identified by "Davies" to have lived mostly during Ramses III's reign.[195] The same author does not rule out completely the probability of ascribing him to a certain "*Ỉpwy*" who might have ended his career at the end of the XIXth dynasty. In conclusion, we would be rather inclined here to hypothesise that there might have been two or more "*Ỉpwy*s" who lived probably at the same time as it could understand from the other "*Ỉpwy*" who was entitled to be *sš ḳd.w* (draftsman, painter, and drawer).[196]

(m) "*N3-ḫy s3 Bw-ḳn-tw.f*" could be safely identified with the workman who appeared in a very wide range of documents (O. DeM 900, O. Černy 7, O. Cairo CG 25873, and P. Berlin P 14448), during Amenmesse's reign.[197]

(n) The name of this workman has occurred once in one of the ostarca of our corpus (KVO 7). His father's name "*Ḫ*ʿ*w*" has occurred in a variety of monuments of Dier el-Medina like TT 214. In this tomb, there was a depiction for his son "*Ḥwy*" as well.[198] What can be ascertained about the both persons is that the two were just ordinary workmen. The son "*Ḥwy*" could have basically lived in the second half of the XIXth dynasty.

(o) It is hard to identify "*Pn-dw3ww*" with certainty as there were many workmen bearing the same name. However, we might be able to confine our endeavour to a certain workman with the same name who occurred in O. Gardiner 87, 7-8. He has also been mentioned on a number of other ostraca dated safely to Amenmesse's reign.[199]

(p) Fortunately, this name is followed by a ranking title "ʿ*3 n is.t*" (the foreman of the gang). According to the chronological charter of Davies, his span of time as "a foreman" could be confined between year 1 of Amenmesse and year 22 of Ramses III.[200] The name of this foreman has been always associated to the left side of the gang.[201]Surprisingly, his name is not mentioned on atop the list, despite the fact that he is the foremost man as for his title.

(q) This name could be restored as "*s3-w3dyt*", the workman who was mentioned on a number of ostraca dated to Amenmesse[202], Seti II[203] and Siptah.[204]

(r) This name could be restored as "*Nfr-ḥtp*", the workman who was the brother of "*N3-ḫy*" and the son of "*Bw-ḳn-tw.f*".[205]

Schematic prosopography:
One of the groundbreaking workmen who can set out a vivid dating framework is "*N3-ḫy* son of *Bw-ḳn-tw.f*". For his first appearance, an allusion is made to Amenmesse's reign.[206] That can be the trigger where we can build on our dating framework. Another workman "*P3-šdw* son of *Ḥḥ-*(*nḫw*)" can be dated from year 2 of Merenptah to the reign of Siptah.[207] In addition, the foreman "*Ḥ3y*" mentioned in this ostracon, can be also securely dated; his lifetime span could be outlined from the beginning of Amenmesse's reign to year 21/22 of Ramses III.[208] Based on the information just cited,

---

[195] Ibid, 152.
[196] Bogoslovsky 1980, 89-116; Wb, 5, 10.17.
[197] Davies 1999, 64, 66.67.
[198] Ibid, 193.
[199] O. Ciaro CG 25779, vso. 6 (year 1); O. Cairo CG 25780, 8, O. Cairo CG 25782 and -83, rto. 7, and rto. 8 (all year 3); O. Cairo 25784, 14-15 (year 4).
[200] Davies 1999, 279.
[201] Ibid, 264.
[202] O. Cairo CG 25779, vso. 8, (year 1).
[203] O. Cairo CG 25512, vso. 1 (year 6).
[204] O. Cairo CG 25516, vso. 26 (year 1).
[205] Davies 1999, 221.
[206] Ibid, 66.
[207] Ibid, 224.
[208] Ibid, 20-21 and 279.

we may set out a date from the reign of Amenmesse to that of Siptah. It follows that KVO 8 may be assigned to the end of the XIXth dynasty. Furthermore, the association of some workcrew names like "*Ỉpwy*", "*s3-w3dyt*" and "*Nfr-ḥtp*" who appeared in a number of documents mostly dated to the end of the XIXth dynasty strengthens this assumption.[209]

[209] O. Cairo CG 25519 (year 1 of Siptah); O. Cairo CG 25520 (Siptah or year 2 of Amenmesse); O. Cairo CG 25522 (Siptah).

KVO 9 (Pl. IX; fig. 9)
O. Cairo JE 72470 (SR 1485)
A day-to-day journal?

Transliteration

(1) *ḥsb.t –rnp.t 2* [...]
(2) *p3y.f ḫn.w*[a] [...]
(3) *Ḥwy*[b] *s3 ḥw(y)-(nfr)* [...]
(4) *Rᶜ-ḥtp*[c] [...]

Translation

(1) Year 2 [...]
(2) His chapel [...]
(3) *Ḥwy* son of *Ḥw(y)-(nfr)* [...]
(4) *Rᶜ-ḥtp* [...]

Commentary

- Dimension: 5.5 x 3.5 cm
- Material: Limestone
- Provenance: Valley of the Kings (Davis' excavations).
- Dating: According to the Special Register, it can assign to the end the XIXth dynasty.
- Condition: In general, the ostracon is in very good condition, despite that fact the left side entirely chipped off. The ink is still vivid and the signs can be transcribed without any difficulty. There is some damage at the top of the ostracon towards the left side which resulted in getting part of the date lost. The ink of the second line is slightly fading and still remains illegible.
- Description: The ostracon is inscribed in black ink and is composed of four lines. The inscriptions have happened to exist only on one side; the other one remains blank however. The fracture which goes along the left side has caused of obscuring, to certain extent, a better understanding to the content of the text.

[a-] With the use of "*ḫn.w*", the content of KVO 9 becomes somewhat problematic. This word used to refer to the the chapel of Ramses II in Deir el Medina which was built by the Ramose and dedicated to this king. [210] Other kings's cults like those of king Seti I were accustomed to being practiced in "*ḫn.w*" despite the fact that he had a sanctuary next to Hathor temple at Deir el Medina.[211] The question which may come across is that: aforementioned cults were undertaken within Deir el Medina community, what is its link to Valley of the Kings where the ostracon in question was found? The fact that there is mentioned "*rnp.t*" may rather attribute KVO 9 to a king and not to a private.We think that there might have built likewise some chapel within the Valley of the Kings. The problem which may stand against this hypothesis is that to which king this chapel was built for. We would not be able to specify any of the kings as we do not have any clue. However, all what we are cetain of is that the ostracon in question is assigned to a regnal year.

As discussed later in this book, some private stelae were erected in the Valley of the Kings (see KVO 19). That might suggest that there could have probably been some chapels for the practice of folk to certain cults. This hint still remains in its pure speculative stage because no assertive archaeological evidences, hitherto, can prove it with certitude.

---

[210] Bruyère 1952, 38, 79, fig. 158.

[211] Jauhiainen 2009, 182.

b- With regard to "*Ḥwy*", we might be able to identify him with the workman whose father is called "*Ḥwy-nfr*".[212] The latter's father is *Nḫt.mnw*[213] mentioned on O. Brussels E. 6311, who was also active by the end of the XIXth dynasty.[214] Collier hints that the first occurrences could be a reference to the chief workman and scribe.[215] "*Ḥwy*" was probably active in the period before as well as his father *Ḥwy-nfr* according to the classification of Collier (Group A).[216]

c- For *Rʿ-ḥtp*, he has appeared in a number of ostraca dated to the end of the XIXth dynasty; between year 1 and 2 of Siptah's reign.[217] He was associated with "*Ḥwy s3 Ḥwy-nfr*" in all these documents. In fact, *Rʿ-ḥtp* can probably be also identified with *(P3)-rʿ-ḥtp*.[218] The spelling of this name is various (or).[219] In the ostracon in question, his name starts off with the determinative without the phonetic signs. All these variants may probably refer to the same name.

For the date of this ostracon, we might be inclined to attribute it to the end of the XIXth dynasty.

Schematic prosopography:

The two workmen, "*Ḥwy* son of *Ḥwy-nfr*" and "*Rʿ-ḥtp*", have been mentioned in a number of ostraca, all attributed to the end of the XIXth dynasty; O. Cairo CG 25519 (year 1 of Siptah), O. Cairo CG 25521 (year 1 or 2 of Siptah), O. Cairo CG 25522 (after year 5 of Siptah), O. Cairo CG 25782 (year 3 of Amenmesse), and KVO 7 (probably year 2 of Siptah's reign). That might help us place this ostracon near the end of the XIXth dynasty or at latest at the beginning of the XXth dynasty. Unfortunately, there are no more assertive clues to help us be more precise than that.

---

212 RPN I, 233.
213 This ostracon is published in Bierbrier 1982, 204, n. 8.
214 Davies 1999, 214.
215 Collier, 2004, xiv.
216 Ibid, 90-91.
217 O. Cairo CG 25521, vso. 2, 10, 11, 12, 16, 17; O. DeM 611 (I 4); and O. Cairo CG 25519, vso. 4, 6, 9.
218 Davies 1999, 44.
219 McDowell 1993, O. Glasgow D. 1925. 66 rt.2-3, 6, pl. Ia.

KVO 10 (Pl. X; fig. 10)
O. Cairo JE Cairo 72471 (SR 1486)
A note of a name?

Transliteration

(1) (?)
(2) <*nswt ḥmt*>

Translation

(1) (?)
(2) <royal wife>

Commentary

- Dimension: 5.5x6 cm
- Material: Limestone
- Provenance: Valley of the Kings (Davis'excavations).
- Dating: According to the Special Register, the ostracon can date to the end of the XIXth dynasty.
- Condition: The ostraocn is in fair condition as well as its ink.
- Description: The ostracon has only one side inscribed in black ink. The inscribed side has two lines; the first is almost lost with the chipping of the stone, leaving some traces for some illegible signs. The second line is still well preserved and legible.

nswt could function as a name or an adjective. Therefore the translation would be "royal wife" or "king's wife".
However, looking over the name written, it can infer that there could be some writing mistakes committed by the scribe. The word "*nswt*" was written in the cartouche not outside as it used to stand. The name of the king referred to is somewhat enigmatic. We know that word "*ḥm.t*" used to have a feminine value. If we look back on the history of the queens who ruled effectively Egypt in the Ramesside Period and held some epithets, we may understand that "Tauesert" could the most plausible one. One of her names is <*sꜣ.t-Rꜥ*> EP. (*ḥnwt*)-*tꜣmri*>.[220] Perhaps the scribe who wrote this ostracon may have intended to write this epithet but probably miswrote it down, mixing "*ḥm.t*" with "*ḥnw.t*". If this hint is correct, we may be able to attribute this ostracon to the end of the XIXth dynasty within (Siptah–Tausert, 1204–1196 B.C.).[221] On the other hand, the name written in the cartouche might mean "royal wife" or "king's wife" making the attribution to a specific period, somewhat difficult.

[220] Beckerath 1999, 162-163.
[221] Bianes & Màlek 1980, 36.

KVO 11 (Pl. XI; fig. 11)
O. Cairo JE 72474 (SR 1489)
A delivery account of firewood

Transliteration "a"

(1) *sš K3r*[a] *n t3 (?)* [...]
(2) *ḫt r*[b] *(t3) ri.t*[c]

Translation "a"

(1) The scribe *K3r* of the (?) [...]
(2) Firewood, a piece of (?) [...]

Transliteration "b"

(1) [...] *iw imi-r mr*[d] *121* [...]
(2) [...] (?) 104 [...]

Translation "b"

(1) [...] woven tissues 121 [...]
(2) [...] (?) 104 [...]

Commentary

- Dimension: a, 3.5x 6 cm, b, 4x 3 cm
- Material: Limestone
- Provenance: Valley of the Kings (Davis' excavations).
- Dating: According to the Special Register, it can date to the end of XXth dynasty.
- Condition: Piece "a" is broken into two pieces however they are glued together. All over the ostracon, there are some black points spread in an uneven intensity. The bigger piece is slightly dappled with these points; however the other piece contains more. Piece "b" is only one smaller slab which has more intensive black points in respect with part "a". These black points have probably emerged as a result of some chemical reactions of the nature of the stone with the outer atmosphere. They get sometimes shape-shifted with the signs themselves and cause somewhat hardship when reading. The state of the ink is still good and readable in spite of these black stains.
- Description: The whole ostracon is inscribed only on one side. Piece "a" contains two incomplete lines; piece "b" is almost the same. It seems that this account was a part of a larger. The handwriting of the two pieces seems to have been written by the same scribe.

Probable dating clue

[a.] The frequency of this name is very rare in the community of workmen. At the beginning, we might probably identify him with a certain guardian called *K3r* who is safely dated to the end of the XXth dynasty.[222] The occurrences of this guardian of the tomb took place mainly by the end of the XXth dynasty.[223] This guardian happened to appear in P. Turin Cat. 2071/224 + 1960, vs 1, 11-1,12.[224] In this papyrus, he was called to present himself in front of the king (*dit iw.f m-bꜣḥ pr-ꜥꜣ*), possibly in order to receive part of the crew's wages. The problem is that here in our ostracon he has the title *sš* not *sꜣw*.[225] In general, the persons who held this title (*sꜣw*) were in charge of receiving salaries in grain along with other workmen; in the accounts of payment they invariably follow the foremen, scribes, and ordinary workmen.[226] We believe that there might have been another person who had the duty of being the guardian of the tomb and whose name constituents were mostly written and not with throwing-stick which in many cases terminates the foreign names.[227] On this ground, we may exclude identifying him with the scribe of the ostracon in question.

Another *Kꜣr* can be identified to be among the subordinates of the chiefs of the Medjay (policemen). His name constituents used to be written: . What we know about *Kꜣriꜣ* (the *mḏꜣy*) is that he was never associated with being the guardian of the tomb neither with being a scribe.

A quarryman was called also *Kꜣr* and his name used to be written .[228] Seeking further in the accounts of Deir el-Medina, we have encountered the same name, without affiliation (O.DeM 45[229], vso. 14, O.DeM 46[230], vso. 14). These ostraca are dated between year 1 and 2 of Ramses IV. The person mentioned on these ostraca might have been the quarryman as usually ordinary workmen were cited on documents without affiliation. Interesting is that the quarryman name's constituents are similar to those the scribe written on this KVO 11. [231] Therefore, we may hypothesize that the quarryman could have probably been the same scribe mentioned on the ostracon in question. The same quarryman could have progressed to occupy the rank of scribe during Ramses II's reign. Thenafter, he held this elevated office. This is not the first time to encounter such a phenomenon in the workmen's community. Janssen has outlined that progress in ranks was characteristic of the hierarchical sphere in Deir el-Medina community.[232] An inferior workman could have had the possibility of promoting himself during the course of his career. On the ground of this brief argument, we may probably be in a position to attribute this ostracon to the reign of king Ramses II or possibly later. Unfortunately, we do not have enough evidences to determine the lifetime span of this workman/ scribe. He might have lived until the end of the XIXth dynasty. In fact, in the inventory records of Cairo Museum, the ostracon is assigned to the end of the XIXth dynasty.

Philological commentary

b. "*ri.t*" means one side of the gang.[233] The initial writing constituents of this word are lost. However, the mention of firewood may help us reconstruct the whole context. This word has occurred in a number of documents (O. Berlin P 10634, 5; O. Qurna 643/1, 3; O. Berlin P 12294). On this ground, we can suggest that what comes before is a preposition "*r*" which means "to".

c. *imi-r-mr* (Wb 2, 96.15;FCD 111; Fischer, Titles, no. 199) is a Ptolemaic title which was used in P. New York MMA 35.9.21, 1 with meaning "weavers or weaving"; the word was written without the determinative.[234] However, in this ostracon, this determinative is lacking here which renders the

---

[222] Häggman 2002, 110, Černy 2004, 159.
[223] O. DeM 44, vso and rto 15; O. DeM 45, vso. 14; O. DeM 46, vso. 14.
[224] KRI VI, 643.
[225] P. BM EA 10375, rto.4, P. Geneva D 407, note on rto. 1, the both are dated within Ramses XI's reign.
[226] Černy 2004, 149.
[227] Ward 1994, 61-85.
[228] Černy 2004, 254. He is mentioned on stela Turin Cat. 1636 and is the owner of the tomb n° 330.
[229] McDowell 1999, 207 no. 156 (translation of obverse 14-17).
[230] Helck 2002, 372-374 (outline of content).
[231] Ibid, 254.
[232] Janssen 1982, 109-113.
[233] Wb 2, 400.4-13; Lesko & Lesko 1982-1990, vol. II, 54; KoptHWb 160, 390.
[234] Smith 2006, 217-232. Quack 2004, 327-332. Goyon 1999, 17-47, col. 1-17.

word problematic in meaning. I would rather inclined to infer a meaning “weaved items” which can fit in here as there is a quantified amount specified by numbers right after that word.

KVO 12 (Pl. XII; fig. 12a, b)
O. Cairo JE 72480 (SR 1495)
A scribal exercise or an account?

Transilteration (*recto*)

8000	*700*	*30*
9000	*800*	*40*
10000	*900*	*50*
20000	*1000*	*60*
30000	*2000*	*70*
40000	*5000*	*80*
(*?*)	*6000*	*90*
	7000	*100*
		100
		200
		300

Translation (*verso*)

50000		60000
60000	100000	70000
70000	200000	80000
80000	300000	90000
90000	40000	(?)
	50000	

Commentary

- Dimension: 10.5 x 7.5 cm
- Material: Limestone
- Provenance: It is attributed to the Valley of the Kings, Davis' excavations.
- Dating: According to the Special Register, it ascribes to the XIX-XXth dynasty,.
- Condition: The top and the bottom are chipped off. The ink is still visible in *recto* and *verso* alike. However, on the *"recto"* the ink of the middle column is slightly effacing. As overall state, the *verso*'s ink is more preserved in respect with that of the *recto*.
- Description: The ostracon has two sides inscribed with black ink. There are three written columns on two sides. The spaces between the columns are well determined and in some points they get irregular.

Classification:
KVO 12 can classify as merely a scribal exercise. That can be understood from the spacing irregularity in the rows' alignments committed by scribe. Moreover, the sequence of numbers is somewhat clumsy and not precise, especially in the "*recto*"; some numbers are repeated twice like "100". We believe that the two sides might have been handwritten by two different scribes. Like Valley of the Kings, from Deir el-Medina there have come some accounts being classified as scribal exercises.[235] A few number of ostraca hold numerals and are found in the Valley of the Kings; O. Cairo CG 25331 was found in the Valley of the Kings with unknown finding spot. Of the unpublished ostraca kept at Cairo

[235] O. DeM 10122; O. DeM 10123.

Museum, we have encountered O. Cairo JE 72473a, b with another exercise of numerals similar to that of KVO 12.

Some considerations:
We have captured until now 4 ostraca on which there are some scribal exercises.[236] Just to give an example, O. Cairo CG 25331 was identified to contain exclusively numerals; it was found in the Valley of the Kings but the date can not be defined.[237] In addition, O. BM EA 65599 + O. BM EA 65600 reverse has been written in 4 columns, starting with more minor numerals; 1, 2 and so forth; we can not assign this ostracon to a specific provenance as it was purchased by N. de Garies Davies in 1923-1924 and then was gifted to the British Museum by W. R. Dawson.[238] Furthermore, O. Cairo JE 72473a, b (unpublished) has the same setting of numerals of the ostracon in question. It was also found in the Valley of the Kings.

Bommas and McDowell alike think that an institutionalized place like "*ʿ3.t sb3y.t*" could have existed in Deir el-Medina where scribes could reproduce, on ostraca, very high standard copies of literary compositions.[239]We wonder whether the Valley of the Kings was such highly secret place in which they required only capable artisans to build and paint royal tombs or it might have been also such a stage on which even minor scribes could play part. In other words, the Valley of the Kings could have been such a place where the beginners of the scribal class could have received some teaching lessons on the hands of the experienced ones. Then, there might have existed some schools throughout the Valley and its lateral small valleys to give such practical lessons to young scribes. That implies that the concentration of some institutions, like school, did not only exist in Deir el-Medina and within temples as usually thought but it might have been found within Valley of the Kings itself.

At the beginning of column 2 (*recto*) there is such sun-disk with sun rays. I have encountered the same sign in O. Cairo JE 72491 (unpublished) classified as Funny-signs ostracon. At the end of line 3 *verso* in KVO 12, there is also an enigmatic sign that I remain unable to interpret. I would rather identify it as a funny-sign as well. Then, we may understand that even the funny-signs could have been integrated into standard-written language, either hieratic or hieroglyphic. In the excavations conducted by Bruyère in 1928, he has discovered a tomb no. 356 of "*Imn-m-wi3*".[240] On the walls, there has been written a "*ḥtp-di-nswt*" funerary formula in which there was inserted after the preposition "*ḥr*" a funny-sign (an eye with lashes found in O. Cairo JE 72491). In conclusion, the non-standard signs recently called funny-signs might have been integrated in standard scripts (hieroglyphic and hieratic alike). The meaning is inherent to its ideographic depiction. With more scrutinized investigation we might get on the track, towards cracking its codes.

---

[236] http://www.wepwawet.nl/dmd/scripts.
[237] Daressy 1901, 84.
[238] Demarée 2002, 39, pls 163-164.
[239] Bommas 2006, 14.
[240] Bruyère 1928, 119.

KVO 13 (Pl. XIII; fig. 13)
O. Cairo JE 71482 (SR 1497)
A note?

Transliteration

(1) [*š3*]*ꜥ m*[a] *inb*[b]

Translation

(1) [From] the enclosure on

Commentary

- Dimension: 9 x 10 cm
- Material: Limestone
- Provenance: Valley of the Kings, Davis's excavations.
- Dating: According to the Special Register, the ostracon can assign to the XIXth dynasty.
- Condition: The overall state of writing is obviously on its way to efface.
- Description: The ostracon is inscribed only on one side and has one line. The beginning of the writing, from the right side, is almost effaced. In fact, it seems unusual to have only one line inscribed on such large limestone slab. The ostracon could have been prepared to receive a larger text and at a certain point it was left out after handing down the first line. There are no other traces for inscription which may reinforce this hint, however.

[a.] "*š3ꜥ-m*" is a compound preposition which means "from (location) to or simply from".[241] During the deciphering process, it was too much hard to recognize the correct reading of this segment. It might shape-shift with as this latter would more fit in here. However, if we transcribe it like that it will make no sense in terms of meaning. "*t3*" is such definite article which precedes feminine nouns. The word "*inb*" is certainly masculine noun and has never had the feminine value.

[b.] "*inb*" could mean "wall, fence, and enclosure" if the word is terminated with .[242] In our case, there is no any determinative. However, it seems more plausible to venture on this meaning as for the preceding preposition. In conclusion, if "wall, fence or enclosure" is the meaning which was wanted to be expressed, there will be a massive range of probabilities to infer what sort of location was. It could refer to a surrounding wall of a royal tomb, an enclosure, a workshop or a hut. These are the most relevant locations which may exist in the Valley of the Kings.

Classification:
For KVO 13, from the single written line, we can infer that this account might have been merely a **note** to indicate to a certain event. The terminology employed through the word "*inb*" suggests that there might have been some wall. The scribe had probably outlined his work, using this ostracon as merely a note to get back to in case of need. Or it might have been just a preparation for a coming work. We have found two ostraca of the Valley of the Kings bearing the same word (O. Cairo CG 25558, vso, 1 and O. Cairo CG 25831, vso, 1). The former was found by Davis in the Valley of the Kings[243] and the latter was discovered by Carter/ Carnarvon to the east side of KV 47 (Siptah), in the

---

[241] Wb 4, 407.8-16; Neveu 1998, 27; Hornung 1991, 218-223, Fig. 154-159; Brunner-Traut 1989, 101-106; Lalouette 1987, 46-52.
[242] Wb 1, 94, 15-95.9; Grapow 1953, 189-209; Assmann 1999, 515-518; Goedicke 1968, 23-26.
[243] Černy 1935a, 101, pl.119.

“Lower stratum” with mark “411” in their excavations of 1922.[244] Against these occurrences of word “*inb*”, there has found none in Deir el-Medina’s accounts, as yet.

[244] Reeves, 331.

KVO 14 (Pl. XIV; fig. 14)
O. Cairo JE72488 (SR 1503)
A jar label

Transliteration

(1) *ḥzb.t-rnp.t 37*[a]

(2) *irp itrw imn.ti*[b]

Translation

1- Regnal year 37
2- Wine of the "Western river"

Commentary

- Dimension: 11x 12.5 cm
- Material: Potsherd
- Provenance: The Valley of the Kings (Carter/ Carnarvon's excavations with mark 285).
- Publication: Černy MSS 111-01
- Dating: The ostracon could safely be assigned to year 37 of Ramses II.
- Condition: The ostracon is in good condition and some written lost parts have been restored from Černy notebook. The writing is slightly fading.
- Description: The ostracon has two written lines in black ink. There are some small red smudges spread on a small part of the ostracon.

[a.] The number 37 mentioned on this ostracon can be a good clue to draw the date. We know that the longest reigning period in the Ramesside Period was that of king Ramses II. He ruled Egypt for about 66 years from around (1290- 1224 B.C.) and none of his successors has ever reached this length of reign.[245] The second ranking king in the Ramesside Period ever went beyond 30 years of reign was king Ramses III; he ruled roughly for about 31 years (1194-1163 B.C.). Therefore, we may be able to ascribe this ostracon to year 37 of king Ramses II; the location in which this ostracon was found may probably support this hypothesis. However, why there was a delivery of wine in year 37 of Ramses II's reign? The answer could be that there might have been a big collective festival in this year to Ramses II himself. It would be difficult to suggest the Sed festival as it is not recorded anywhere that Ramses II had held it in this year.[246]

Geographical site

[b.] "*itrw imn.*t"i is a topographical term which refers to a location at the north-western Nile Delta region; it is located where there is the modern Alexandria now.[247]It was a place where they could produce the wine and transport it to different places throughout Egypt. The most testamentary evidence for that are Malqata's ostraca in which it is stated explicitly that the wine was produced at this place.[248] Ogdon thought that the earlier orthographical form of "*itrw imn.ti*" during the Old Kingdom was "*mr imntt* (-

[245] Baines & Malek 1990, 36.
[246] Hornung & Stähelin 2006, 71-72.
[247] McGovern 1996, 69-108.
[248] Winlock 1912, 184-90; Winlock 1915, 253-6; Lansing 1918, 8-14; Hayes 1951, 35-56, 82-111, 156-83, 231-42.

nfr.t)", Canal of the beautiful (Goddess) of-the-West.[249] Leahy has hinted on a reading of some jar labels of Malqata in which it is mentioned also "*itrw imn.ti*" that the name of the place could be assigned to the reign of Ramses II; in this context the wine was described as "good" in quality. He might probably be correct in his hint.[250] Malqata site was probably used also as an administrative place where there could have been some delivery of items to be consumed on certain events. Further evidence which attests the designation "*itrw imn.ti*" is the jar labels dated to Ramses II'reign and found at the Ramesseum. They are held now in "L'Institut d'égyptologie de Strasbourg".[251] On 26 amphorae from the Annex of king Tutankhamun, the estates and the vineyards are situated there as well.[252] In the Nineteenth dynasty, it was claimed that there does not exist any sort of attestation in which the "*itrw imn.t*" is mentioned, except some citation to some places in Delta, oases and south of Egypt where Ramses III planted vineyards and used vintners and labours from the class of his foreign captives.[253]That means that this ostracon would, hitherto, be one of the first attestations where this place (*itrw imn.t*) is cited in the XIXth dynasty documentary material. In the Twentieth dynasty, Gardiner published a squatting statue in Cairo Museum whose owner held the titles "*the scribe of the dispatches of the Lord of the two Lands, overseer of the treasury of Amun, and the great steward in the Western-river*".[254]

---

[249] Ogdon 1978-1979, 65-73, 5 fig.
[250] Leahy 1978, 14-15, no. 61, 65, 68, pl. 6a, 7.
[251] Bouvoier 2003, 193-194, 198, 200, 206 (n. 1257).
[252] Černy 1965, 1-4, 21-4, pls. i-v.
[253] From Papyrus Harris (1, 7, 10 ff) in Breasted 1907, sections 151-412.
[254] Gardiner 1948, 19-22.

KVO 15 (Pl. XV; fig. 15)
O. Cairo JE 72489 (SR 1504)
A jar label

Transliteration

(1) (?) *nfr nfr*[a] *n pꜣ bꜥḥw*[b]
(2) [*ḥm.f*][c] *ꜥnḫ* (*w*) *wḏꜣ* (*w*) *snb* (*w*) *r*-[(*ḫ*)*t*[d] *nswt*] *ms*

Translation

(1) An excellent (?) of the inundated lands
(2) [His Lord] L.P.H under [the authority of] ms

Commentary

- Dimension: 10x 14.5 cm
- Material: Potsherd
- Provenance: Valley of the Kings (Carter/ Carnarvon's excavations of 1922 with mark 345).
- Cft. Černy MSS 111-01.
- Dating: According to the Special Register, it could be assigned to the XIX-XXth dynasty.
- Condition: The ink is effacing and the written surface is flaking off.
- Description: The ostracon is consisted of two lines. The first one is relatively well-preserved; however the second one is almost gone. We relied basically on the manuscript of Černy to restore the lost parts of the transcription.

a. *nfr nfr* is a designation which describes wine quality. A considerable number of jar labels from the Ramesseum have the "*irp*" being qualified by "*nfr nfr*".[255] This designation usually implies that the wine is from high quality. However, in the transcription, there appears a "*t*" which renders the whole word somewhat difficult. We know that word "*irp*" was never terminated with "*t*".

Geographical sites:
b. "*bꜥḥw*"[256] means "flood" or "inundation" as it is translated by Sceknkel in *"Bewässerungsrev*".[257] He mentioned, depending on Moꜥallah's sources, that the term may rather refer to the flooding process.[258] "*bꜥḥw*", in KVO 15, could refer to a geographical term which indicates to a certain site in Upper Egypt rather than to the inundation process as meaning.

Restoring some parts:
c. "*ḥm.f*" could be restored as a usual formula which was commonly used in the jar labels of Malqata. In fact, Leahy could restore the missing word which precedes the stative formulae "L. P. H" with "*ḥm.f*" or sometimes with (*tpy n ḥm.f*). The mentioning of "L. P. H" would hint that there was an important occasion to take place in the Valley of the Kings.[259] Unfortunately, the item delivered on this occasion is quite effaced and we can't get an approach of it. There might have been written wine which was frequently delivered on certain occasions; however it could have been also beer, fat, or oil. However, we may advocate the word "wine" as for the following adjective which used to be associated with wine.
Meaning of some word:

---

255 Bouvoier 2003, 226-234.
256 Meeks 1978, 124.
257 Schenkel 1978, 51.
258 Mo'alla 1a3; Davies 1902, pl. XXV, 23 (= URK. VII 178, 16),
259 Leahy 1978, *passim*.

d. "*r-ḫt*" is an expression which means "under the authority of".[260] In its orthographical appearance, it can be followed by a name of a high ranking official, and was frequently used in association with estates (specifically lands).[261]

---

[260] Lesko & Lesko 1982-1990, vol. II, 52; Gardiner 1937, 1, 2, 3.
[261] Valbelle 1976, 102. This article focuses on the difference between the use of "*r-ḫt*" and "*m-ḏr.t*".

KVO 16 (Pl. XVI; fig. 16)
O. Cairo JE 72501 (SR 1516)
A note (?)

Transliteration

(1) *ꜥꜣ nry*

Translation

(1) The great of Terror

Commentary

- Dimension: 5 x 11 cm
- Material: Limestone
- Provenance: Valley of the Kings (Carter/ Carnarvon's excavations of 1922 with mark 292).
- Dating: The ostracon is dated, according to the Special Register of Cairo Museum, to the XIX-XXth dynasty. The epithet cited, may probably set this ostracon at Seti II's reign. The fact that this ostracon was found at the entrance of KV 9 (Ramses VI).
- Condition: the ink is in very good condition.
- Description: the ostracon is inscribed only with one line written in black ink on one side. It does not sound that there are other missing part of writing. In other words, the ostracon was inscribed to receive only this line.

In fact, the only king in the Late XIXth dynasty who had ever taken over this epithet is king Seti II; he was entitled or "the great of Terror in all Lands".[262] In KVO 6, he is entitled also the "the Lord of the Terror". It seems that this king in particularly used frequently to associate the epithet "*nry*" to his name. So, we may probably attribute this ostracon to his reign. However, the finding spot (Ramses VI) remains an obstacle for this attribution.

[262] Beckerath 1999, 161.

KVO 17 (XVII; fig 17a, b)
O. Cairo JE 72502 (SR 1517)
List of high ranking titles

Transliteration (*recto*)

	ḥry- [*i͗*]*ḥw*[e]	
	ḥry-mḏꜣy[f]	
	ḥry-bi͗t[g]	
	[*ḥry-i͗-*(*nf*) *ww*][h]	
[*ḥry-ẖꜣ*(*w.t*)][n]		[*ḥry*]-*mz*[a] *b*
[*ḥry*]		[*ḥry*]-*i͗s.t*[b]
	ḥry-[*mz wdn.w*][i]	*ḥry-pr-šnꜥ* [c]
	ḥry-[*ẖꜥḳ*][j]	*ḥry*-[*mr*][d]
	ḥry-nw.w[k]	
	ḥry-[*bꜣky.w*][l]	
	ḥry-[*ꜥẖ.w*][m]	

Translation (*recto*)

	The superior of the stable	
	The superior of the police	
	The superior of the bees	
	[The superior of the sailors]	
[The superior of the offering tables]		[The superior] of the (?) carriers
[The superior]		[The superior] of the gang
	The superior of [the offering bearers]	The superior of the storehouse
	The superior of [the barbers]	The superior of [servants]
	The superior of the hunters	
	The superior of [the royal works]	
	The superior of [brewers]	

Transliteration (*verso*)

[*imi-r- nw.w*][o]
[*im.i-r mr*][p]
[*imi-r k3.t*][q]

[(*s*)*smt*]

imi-r st[r]
imi-r iḥ(*.w*)[s]

Translation (*verso*)

[The overseer of the hunters]
[The overseer of the *mr*]
[The overseer of the building activity]

[Horses] (*?*)

The overseer of the storehouse
The overseer of the cattle

Commentary

- Dimension: a, 10 x 14 cm; b, 5.5 x 6.5 cm
- Material : Limestone
- Provenance: Valley of the Kings. The smallest piece is designated Carnarvon/300.
- Cft. Černy's MSS (106.21), transcription only.
- Dating: According to the Special Register, the ostracon could date to the XIXth dynasty. As for KVO 17, it is difficult to attribute this ostracon to a specific period of time as there is no any clue for dating. On fragment "b", there is written number "300"; one of the numerical designations of Carter/Carnarvon excavations. That can help us trace down the finding spot of this ostracon. According to sources, fragment "300" was found beside the entrance of KV 9 of Ramses VI.[263] That might probably prompt us to put KVO 17 somewhere within the reining period of that king. Accordingly, KVO 17 might probably assign to the first half of the XXth dynasty (1151-1143 B.C). The bulk of the ostraca found at that site is dated in terms of palaeographical basis, to rather the XIXth dynasty.[264] The bulk of ostraca discovered at the place where this ostracon was found is not assigned to king Ramses VI. That may undermine our initial ascription of KVO 17 to the XXth dynasty. Another ostracon designated "O. Cairo CG 25760" discovered by the same excavators, Carter/ Carnarvon in the Valley of the Kings, holds the same account. O. Cairo CG 25760 is safely dated to Ramses II's reign.[265] On palaeographical basis, the handwriting of the the ostracon in question assimiliates that of O.

[263] Reeves 1990, 328.
[264] O. Cairo CG 25802 (first half of XIXth dynasty); O. Cairo CG 25805 (middle of XIXth dynasty); O. Cairo CG 25809 (first half of XIXth dynasty); O. Cairo CG 25815a, b (middle of XIXth dynasty); O. Cairo CG 25832a, b, c (second half of XIXth dynasty); look these ostraca up in Černy 1935b, 93-101.
[265] KRI III, 642-643.

Cairo CG 25760. They might have been written by the same scribe. So that may set the XIXth dynasty, within Ramses II's reign, as a probable date to KVO 17.

- Condition: The material of the stone is still well preserved. However, the ink of the biggest piece "a" is effacing notably*; recto* an*d verso* alike.
- Description: The ostracon is clearly broken into three pieces. Since the biggest piece's ink is effacing remarkably, we relied on the Černy's notes in which there is only transcription of this ostracon. The "*recto* a, b" is consisted of three columns; however the "*verso* a, b" is only two.

There is a distinction in functioning between "*ḥry*" and "*ỉmi-r*". We are used to knowing that "*ỉmi-r*" is higher in ranking than "*ḥry*". The earliest attested title connected with the treasury is "*ḥry-pr ḥḏ*". It was attested as early as the reign of king Den. In the Third dynasty, the office was held by an overseer, or *ỉmi-r pr-ḥḏ*, a title borne by *Nfr*, *Mry*, and *Pḥ-r-nfr*, who also held three other titles connected with the treasury. Simultanesouly the overseer of the "white house" could hold the tenure of the office of the granaries.[266] After that it was widespread during the Old Kingdom with variety of tasks (Wb 1, 74.13; Jones, Titles OK, no. 255).[267]For Gardiner, as a ranking title, perhaps "*wr*" is higher than "*ḥry*". He thinks that "*ḥry*" could be translated as "captain".[268]However, we would be more inclined here to translate it as "superior" that is the literal translation of this word in "Wb 3, 141.14-142.2".

We shall handle here the titles one by one to understand the real function of each. We would not be able to ascertain that the titles are cited in hierarchal sequence.

a. "*ḥry-mz b(?)*" is written incomplete; its second constituent which starts off with "*b*" is unfortunately lost. However, we know that "*mz*" is associated with those who held a post as "carriers".[269] Therefore, the word has been very often written with phonogram " " in combination with " ". The latter gives the implication of motion and the verb "*mz*" itself has the meaning "to bring". The whole title would be best translated "the superior of (?) carriers.

b. "*ḥry-is.t*" is translated as the "the Captain of the crew" in "Ward".[270]This title has occurred in "O. Cairo CG 25764".[271] It is an ostracon discovered by Davis in 1905-06, on which there was attested a series of titles for the "Servant of the Place of Truth *K3-nḫt*". O. Cairo CG 25764 can date from the end the XXth to the beginning of XXIst dyansty.

c. "*ḥry-šnʿ*" may mean the "the Master of the Storehouse" in "Ward".[272] It has been, in many cases, translated with this meaning.[273]

d. "*ḥry-mr.(t)*" might probably be restored hieroglyphic to be [ ]; in Wb.2 106.20 it is written . This title means "the Master of Servants".[274] It has occurred in P. BM EA 75015 (*recto* 8); it dates to the Late XXth dynasty. [275]

e. "*ḥry-iḥ.w*" can perhaps be translated as "Stable Master".[276] It is a title which has been widely used during the Ramesside Period.[277] It appeared in O. BM EA 50730 + O. BM EA 50745 which is dated to dynasty XX, first year of Ramses VI.[278] This ostracon was purchased by the British Museum from M. Mohassib in 1912.

f. "*ḥry-mḏ3y*" can be translated the "Chief of the Police".[279] We know that the "Police" were those Nubian Nomads in the Old and the Middle Kingdom; this can justify the writing of thc "throwing

---

[266]M. Parsons, Ancient Egyptian Government and Bureaucracy. Available On: http://www.touregypt.net/featuresstories/government.htm.

[267] Kanawati 2002, 42-45, pl. 1b, 17-21, 53, 55b.

[268] Gardiner 1947, 84, 86.

[269] Wb 2, 135.22-23.

[270] Ward 1982, 115.965.

[271] Černy 1935b, 81, 94 ; Daressy1922, 75 and 76.

[272] Ward 1982, 123.1045.

[273] Vogelsang & Gardiner 1908, 6-7 and pl. 5-17; Gardiner 1923, 5-25; E. Wente 1967, 24.

[274] Ward 1982, 118.992; Sweeney 2001, 175-6.

[275] Demarée 2006, 7-9, 34-37 (photographs, transcription, translation, commentary).

[276] Wb 1, 121.7; Lesko & Lesko 1982-1990, vol. II, 131.

[277]Helck 1963; KRI I, 45-58.

[278] Helck 2002, 440-441 (translation).

[279] Wb 2, 186.12.

stick" as determinative which signifies people with foreign origins.[280] They had been rather on warlike with Egypt than on Peaceful terms. By the beginning of the XVIIIth dynasty, they helped Egypt release itself from the Hyksos invasion. In the Ramesside time, they were actually in good relation with the authority in such a way that they could be smoothly integrated in western Thebes's desert defence forces.[281] By the increase of the workforce number during Ramses IV up to 120 workmen, the number of the Police was uplefted to be 60 chiefs.[282]

g. "*ḥry-bit*" could mean the "superior of the Bee-keepers". This title was associated rather with the word "*imi-r*" during the Old and the Middle Kingdoms. There were actually the "the Overseer of the Bee-Keepers and the Overseer of the Bee-keepers of the entire Land" [283]

h. This title could probably correspond to "*ḥry-i-nf.ww*" which means the "Commander of the Sailors"[284] or "Chief Skippers"[285]. It can be found in Al. Ayedi (397.1337), written . It is the fisrt time we ever find such title in documents from Valley of the Kings.

i. "*mz-wdn.w*" means the "Offerings Bearer".[286] The combination "*ḥry mz-wdn.w*" has never been attested in any of the documentary texts of either Deir el-Mednia or the Valley of the Kings. However, the word "*wdn*" was mentioned on two ostraca O. DeM 10026[287] and O. UC 39658[288]. The latter's provenance is completely unknown.

j. "*ḥry ḫꜥḳ*" is such title which never occurred in any document neither from Deir el-Medina nor from the Valley of the Kings. The Barber-staff as a word long existed since the Old Kingdom.[289]

k. "*ḥry nw.w*" is another title which has never been cited in any of the documents of Valley of the Kings neither in that of Deir el-Medina. "*nwi*" or "*nww*" could mean the "Crew of Hunters".[290] The title was mostly in association with "*imi-r*" being during the Middle Kingdom.[291] Their mention was in close combination with "*mḏꜣy*" and the word itself was terminated with the determinative of the "foreign lands".[292] Perhaps the both staffs had the same Nubian origins.[293]

l. "*ḥry-bꜣk.w*" could mean the "Superior of the Workers"; the meaning is very general- it could be the "Superior of the king Workers or some private Workers".[294] I

m."*ḥry-ꜥḫw*" could probably mean the "the Superior of the vessels-beer Porters (brewers)".[295] This combination of words has never occurred in any of the documents of the Valley of the Kings. "*ꜥḫ*" could mean the "vessel of the beer"; written and dated to the XVIIIth dynasty.[296] On the ostracon in question, the determinative is and group of people. Therefore, it would be plausible to think that the meaning of the word could be "vessel-beer Porters". In fact, the same occurrence of the word could be found in O. Berlin P 14885 (line 7).[297]

n. "*ḥry ḫꜣ(w.t)*" is written incomplete, but could probably be restored in this manner. For Lapp, it could be translated as the "Master of the offering tables".[298]

---

280 Gardiner 1947 I, 73, and II, 269.
281 Černy 2004, 261.
282 Ibid, 262.
283 Ward 1982, 21.130-31.
284 Wb 2, 251.7.
285 Radwan 1987, 223-28, PL.III.
286 Wb 2, 135.23; Gardiner 1947 I, 63.
287 Grandet, 2006, 32, 215 (photograph, facsimile, transcription, description, transliteration, translation).
288 Černy & Gardiner 1957, 10 (description) and pl. 33-33A no. 4 (facsimile and transcription of obverse).
289 Wb 3, 365.3-4; Jonesv 2000, no. 2822.
290 Wb. 2-19.
291 Ward 1982, 226.
292 Ward 1982, 822.
293 Gardiner 1947 I, 84*.
294 Wb. 1, 430.4.
295 Al-Ayedi 2006, 375, 1261.
296 Wb 1, 221-16.
297 http://obelix.arf.fak12.uni-muenchen.de/cgibin/mmcgi2mmhob/mho1/p_new_user?user=gast&pw=DeMonline.
298 Lapp 1997, pl. 2-9; Wb 3, 226.18; Ayedi, Titles NK, no. 1352.

o. "*imi-r nw.w*" means the "overseer of the hunters".[299] This title has never been attested in any of Valley of the Kings' documents (see note "k").
p. "*imi-r mr(?)*" can not be easily restored as the second part of the second word could hold large range of probabilities.
q. The title of the « the overseer of the work » has very ancient tradition. The word "*k3.t*" is translated normally as "work", its nature includes activities of construction, manual activities, and transportation of material.[300] For this reason, during the New Kingdom, the title still refers to the responsibilities of public building tasks, but also to manual and transporting work as illustrated in the Theban tombs.[301] In his study about groups of titles of the New Kingdom, Steimann puts in evidence that the "*imi-r k3.t*" could be attributed to people of diverse ranks, implying a different value of the title. It can vary from the highest rank of the administration like the vizier down to the lower officials like local administrators.[302] During the New Kingdom, the simple version of the title is attested for many officials. That may underline what Aling has suggested: "this is not a designation of rank or office, but indicates that the bearer supervised construction work at one time or at one place" .[303] The nature of this title can imply extreme diversification and Specialization in different fields of the administrative structure.[304]
r. "*imi-r st*" means the "overseer of the storehouse". [305]
s. "*imi- r iḥ(.w)*" means the "overseer of the cattle".[306]

Some important notes:
As a matter of fact, this ostracon was found in the Valley of the Kings. All the cited titles correspond to diverse functions being born by some officials. That may imply that the Valley of the Kings was not such place in which everything was dedicated to the construction works of the royal tombs. However, there might have probably been such a small community in which different organizations were interacting under a local headquarter.
Ventura suggested that the Royal valleys, and particularly the Valley of the Kings, were august, secret, concealed, guarded and unapproachable sites.[307] From our perspective, the Valley of the Kings could have been an active, accessible and interactive, cosmopolitan community. For instance, KVO 17 contains a spectrum of combinations of titles that have never been attested together in one document from the Valley of the Kings. When mentioned "*imi-r iḥ.w*", it certainly comes to mind that the temple had been long associated with animals in general. The animals, especially cows, could have been involved in agricultural activities to cultivate the fields of the memorial temple.[308] They were also used for cultivation purposes by the necropolis workmen in the Deir el-Medina community. That may bring up a logical question: was there some real administrative institution, like a temple, in the Valley of the Kings? This question may not be affirmatively answered now as there are no assertive archaeological evidences as yet. However, the titles listed up on KVO 17 like "*ḥry-ḫ3(w.t)*" and "*ḥry-mz-wdn.*w", are an allusion to a somewhat well-equipped community, its different bodies were in harmony under a larger local headquarter. This community was probably in association with some other institutions based somewhere in the Valley of the Kings and there may have been considerable interaction. "*ḥry-ḫʿḳ*" or the "chief of the barbers" is a very characteristic title of inhabited centers. The word "*ḥry*" and "*imi-r*" as significance imply that there should have been subordinates. This means that there was a team of barbers, similar to other teams for different jobs, undertaking their work within the Valley of the Kings. The finding of several huts spread throughout the entire Valley of the Kings, and in its side-valleys, suggests that there may have been inhabitable installations. That

---

299 Wb 3, 226.18; Al-Ayedi 2006, no. 1352.
300 Wb 5 98,2-101, 8.
301 Steinmann1980, 137-157, part. 144-146.
302 For a study about the different rank of the same title see : Vernus, 1994, 251-260.
303 C.f. Aling 1976, 55.
304 Al-Ayedi 2006, 135-153.
305 Wb 4, 2.17-18; Ward, 1982, no. 313.
306 Wb 1, 119.21; Jones 2000, no. 286.
307 Ventura 1986, 170.
308 Haring 1997, 255.

would have forced the central administration to construct enough dwelling extensions to contain such increase of workmen. This phenomenon has occurred sometime during Ramses IV's reign.

KVO 18 (Pl. XVIII; fig. 18a, b)
O. Cairo JE 72503 (SR 1518)
A list of Ramses II sons' names

Transliteration (*recto)*

(1)*s3-nsw (?)*
(2) *s3-nsw s3-ptḥ*[a]
(3) *s3-nsw snẖt-n-imn*[b]
(4) *s3-nsw Mry-mn-tiw*[c]
(5) *s3-nsw Rʿ-mry*[d]
(6) *s3-nsw I*[*?*]
(7) *s3-nsw*[*?*]

Translation (*recto)*

(1) Prince ?
(2) Prince "*s3-ptḥ*"
(3) Prince "*snẖt-n-imn*"
(4) Prince "*Mry-mn-tiw*"
(5) Prince "*Rʿ-mry*"
(6) Prince [?]
(7) Prince [?]

Transliteration (*verso*)

(1) *s3-nsw ʿ3m sw*[e]
(2) *s3-nsw sš-sw*[f]
(3) *s3-nsw Wr-m3*[g]
(4) *s3-nsw st-m-tn*[h]
(5) *s3-nsw Nb-n*[i]
(6) *s3-nsw I*[*?*]
(7) *s3-nsw*[*?*]
(8) *s3-nsw sw-ty*[j]
(9) *s3-nsw Rʿ-msw-p3 it-nṯr*[k]

Translation (*verso)*

(1) Prince [*?*]
(2) Prince "*sš-nsw*"
(3) Prince "*Wr-m3*"
(4) Prince "s*t-m-*(*ḥr?*)"
(5) Prince "*Nb-n*"
(6) Prince *I*[*?*]
(7) Prince [?]
(8) Prince "*sw-ty*"
(9) Prince "*Rʿ-msw-p3 it-nṯr*"

Commentary

- Dimension: 14.5 x 20 cm
- Material: Limestone
- Provenance: Valley of the Kings (Carter/Carnarvon's excavations with mark 301).

- Dating: For the Special Register, it can date to the XIXth dynasty.
- Conditions: It is consisted of two four slabs. They had been glued all together by a certain scholar (probably Černy). The ink of the upper two pieces of the *verso* is still well-preserved and legible in comparison with the lower two ones. The ink of the *recto* is well-preserved. The ostracon is chipped off in several parts, especially on the edges. Even though, the ostracon is in very good status along with its inscription.
- Description: Both the *recto* and *verso* are written in black ink. The *recto* is consisted of 7 inscribed lines. There is very large space running from up to bottom and left blank without inscription. However, the left side holds all the princes' names. The *verso* is inscribed in 9 lines and the right side is also left without inscription; all the names are inscribed on the left one. There might have been a big slab, chipped off with some names. This can not apply on the *recto* as most of the names are fortunately preserved except the last two lines at the bottom.

We would rather prefer to write the names of king Ramses II's sons transliterated in order to avoid any sort of misunderstanding. That is not applied to famous names like Merenptah as he could ascend the throne and become a real governing king.

[a-] "*sꜣ-ptḥ*" could be identified with the prince "Siptah" represented in Wadi es-Sebua, the inner Court, base register. He is there depicted wearing a wig and side lock with straight bottom. His right hand is raised in adoration attitude; left hand: fan over shoulder.[309] In (KRI II 866.13), the places of the princes occupy 26 through 30 along this wall and this king takes over place number 26.[310] His name on Wdi-es-Sebua is mentioned among princes Siamun, Siatun, and Montuenheqau. His burial like all the other sons of king Ramses II might have been located in tomb KV 5 where there are now the ongoing excavations conducted by Weeks Kent.[311] This tomb was presumably going to receive multi burials of the sons of king Ramses II as for the multi-rooms existing therein. The *sꜣ-ptḥ* is mentioned in Abydos, temple of Seti I, first court, west wall, south side.[312] His name is stated fully on a block statue kept in Louvre under inventory no. E 25413 (published by Vandier).[313] He claims in this article that the statute could have probably been made in the reigning period of king Ramses II as for the crude style of carving. However, he does not consider him as the son of king Ramses II. On the other hand, Kitchen is the only scholar who attributes him as a son of king Ramses II.[314]

[b.] For "*snḫt-n-imn*", little is known about him. His name's occurrences can be counted as follows: Wadi es-Sebua, inner court, south and north walls, base register; Ramesseum, Hypostyle hall, west wall, south and north sides; temple of Seti I, west wall, south side.[315] He is classified as prince number 20.[316] However in KVO 18, he is mentioned right after the name of prince Siptah who has got the 26th ranking position among Ramses II's sons.

[c.] "*Mry-mn-tiw*" was represented in Wadi es-Sebua, inner court, north wall, base register. He might be the prince number 29 on Abydos list.[317] His representation on Abydos list can be located in the temple of Seti I, first court, south wall, and south side. [318] His name on this list is fragmented and only part is left. We can notice here the slight difference in the orthographical shape between the use of "*tiw*" and "*ṯ*". This is because there was a sound change of the consonant which was amended by Middle Egyptian.[319] He is scarcely mentioned in publication except in (KRI 867. 16).[320]

---

[309] Fisher 2001, 17, p.4.26.

[310] Ibid, vol. I, 118.

[311] Weeks 2000, *passim*. This a part of the Theban Mapping Project.

[312] Fisher 2001, p.26.1-4.

[313] Vandier 1971, 165-91.

[314] KRI II 859.9; KRI II 907.15-908.8. The latter was just a response to oppose Vandier's point of view and attribute the block statue of Ramses-Siptah to being one of the sons of king Ramses II.

[315] Fisher 2001, vol. II, 178, 20.1-6.

[316] KRI II 865. 16, 866.1-2 and 16, 868.1; PM VI 3 (10)- (11).

[317] Fisher 2001, vol II, 18, 4.29.

[318] Ibid, 52, p.15.5.

[319] Allen 2000, 20.

[d.] "*Rꜥ-mry*" is a prince who was frequently depicted in many royal processions. In Abu Simbel, small temple, façade, first colossus from south[321] and north[322] ends. Elsewhere he is depicted in Wadi es-Sebua, inner court, south and north walls, base register. In addition, he is represented in the Ramesseum, hypostyle hall, west wall, south and north sides. In Luxor Temple, however he is depicted in several places; first pylon, inner side, court Ramses II, north wall, east side; at the same Temple at Ramses II court, the interior west and south wall, north side; at the same court of Ramses II, exterior south and west wall.[323]

[e.] For the name of this prince, I have been unable to decipher it as there are several probabilities. Therefore, I prefer to avoid getting into detail.

[f.] "*sš-nsw*" is rather a title than a proper name of one of Ramses II's sons. We know that among the sons of king Ramses II, his son Merenptah was mostly associated with this title. In Gebel l- Silsila, chapel of Horemhab, north doorway in front of Chapel of Pesiur, he was depicted with this title and .[324] On a grey granite block coming from Athribis (Benha)-Tell Atrib (JE 32009), Merenptah's name was written with the same title.[325] On a red granite colossus of king Ramses II (CGC 575), Merenptah's name was incised by the left leg of king Ramses II along with his titles, among which there is also the royal scribe.[326] There is a grey granite plinth, kept in Florence Museum under inventory no.1681 (1801), on which there is once more the depiction of the same prince.[327] There is a black granite colossal statue of Sesostoris I kept at Cairo Museum with SR. 634, and usurped by Merenptah, on which there is a depiction for the same prince offering to Seth. On this statute, there is incised the same title "the royal scribe".[328] From all these citations, we may be in a position to assign this name to the prince and the king Merenptah.

[g.] "*Wr-mꜣ*" may probably be rather a title which refers to an official position than to a proper name. This title had been frequently written on several Mastabas from the Old Kingdom and was mostly associated with Heliopolis.[329] The title was born by the priests of Heliopolis and means (the great seer, D. Jones, Titles Old Kingdom, no. 1429). One of Ramses II's sons might probably have been in charge of this post at *Ꞽwn.w*. What may support this hypothesis is that this "title" has been mentioned only on KVO 18 and nowhere else on Ramses II sons' lists.

[h.] "*st-m-(ḥr?)*" is completely unknown name whose occurrence can be found on the ostracon in question. The reading of the sign after "*m*" is hardly decipherable. However, we may be able to define this as rather title than a proper name. It might be the title which was held by the Sem-priests, written sometimes (Wb 4, 119, W. Ward, Titles, no. 168).[330]

[i.] "*Nb-n*" could probably be another title which means simply "the lord of....". It is also mentioned only on KVO 18.

[j.] "*sw-ty*" might be identified with Sethi who was also present at Kadesh and Dapur. He was buried in KV5 – where two of his canopic jars were found – around Year 53. On his funerary equipment his name is spelled *"sw-ty"*.

[k.] "*Rꜥ-msw-pꜣ it-nṯr*" is mentioned only on KVO 18. "*iti-nṯr*" means god's father and is a priestly title which was long held across the whole Pharaonic Period (Wb 1, 142. 1-6, 8; Jones, Titles O.K no.

---

320 Gauthier 1914, 98 NO. 24. He restores the name as Simontu rather than *"Mry-mntiw"*; however, in Kitchen he restores it as *"Mry-mntiw* ".

321 PM VII (1) ; KRI II 766.8; Champollion 1835-1845, pl. IX.

322 PM VII (6); KRI II 766.15 ; Champollion 1835-1845, pl. IX.

323 Fisher 2001, vol II, 156-158; PM II 333 (202); KRI 171.14.

324 KRI II 385.11; Gomaà1973, cat. 76.

325 PM IV 66; Engelbach 1930, 197-202.

326 Hourig 1989, 21-22.

327 PM IV 22; Christophe 1951, 335-72.

328 KRI 902.15-903.2.

329 PM III, 47-179: Giza, West Field: Mastaba of *Wn-s-ḫt* (G 4840); PM III, 47-179: Giza, West Field: Mastaba of *Mr-ib* (G 2100 I-annex); PM III, 47-179: Giza, West Field: Mastaba of *Sšꜣt-ḥtp*, gen. *Ḥty* (G 5150), double statue.

330 For further verification on the orthographical appearance of this word see Lesko & Lesko 1982-1990, vol III, 45.

1283; Ward, Titles, no. 570 e). Therefore, we may identify the *verso* of this ostracon as just a document which holds rather titles than proper names.

Notes:

Since KVO 18 was found beside the entrance of KV 9 of king Ramses VI, it would have made sense attributing it to this king. However, the major part of the ostraca found along with this ostracon at this place, were ascribed to the reign of king Ramses II. For example, O. Cairo CG 25815a[331], O. Cairo CG 25809[332], O. Cairo CG 25816, O. Cairo CG 25807[333], O. Cairo CG 25813[334], O. Cairo CG 25802[335] are all assigned to Ramses II's reign. There could have probably been there a workshop where workmen could execute Ramses II's royal works. It could have been written somewhere in the reigning course of king Ramses II to be copied onto one of tombs (it could have been KV 5).

[331] KRI III, 567 (transcription) ; Černy 1935b, 96, 117, pl. CXII (description, transcription and facsimile).

[332] Helck 2002, 64-65 (translation); KRI III, 514 (transcription); Černy 1935b, 95, 116, pl. CXII (description, transcription and facsimile).

[333] KRI II, 233 (transcription); KRI II, 86 (translation); KRI notes II, 145-146 (commentary).

[334] Kitchen1982, 191 (translation); KRI III, 569 (transcription); Helck 2002, 59 (translation).

[335] KRI III, 531 (transcription); Černy 1935b, 93, 114, pl. CX (description, transcription and facsimile).

KVO 19 (Pl. XIX; fig. 19)
O. Cairo JE 72504 (SR 1519)
A draft of a stela

Transliteration

ḥtp di nsw	*3ḫ ikr*[a]	*n R*ʿ *Ḥrw*[b] *m3*ʿ *ḫrw*

Translation

An offering that king gives	The beneficent soul	of *R*ʿ *Ḥrw* justified

Commentary

- Dimension: 9.5x 10.5 cm
- Material: Limestone
- Provenance: Valley of the Kings (Carter/ Carnarvon's excavations with mark 371).
- Dating: According to the Egyptian Museum Special Register, it can attribute XIX-XXth dynasty.
- Publication: Demarèe 1983, 31-32, pl. Ix.
- Condition: The ostracon is in very good condition with a big lost part towards the bottom. The ink of the ostracon is still clear and legible. This also can be applied to the figure drawn on the ostracon from which there remains the bust.
- Description: The ostracon is inscribed only on one side and has three columns. The ink is black and the overall handwriting is clear and easily legible. There is a figure of a man down toward the bottom of the ostracon. It seems that the ostracon was destined to be just a draft for a funerary stela. There is a horizontal line border which runs across the whole ostracon.

[a.] "*3ḫ ikr*" is such an expression which should be explained, word by word, in order to understand the significance of its derivation. During the Old Kingdom, In the Pyramid Texts, there was no any citation to this term; however about the "*3ḫ*", there were so many quotations.[336] For the "*3ḫ*", it is connected to the divine world and the Hereafter.[337] There is a quite strict link between the "*3ḫ*" and both gods "*R*ʿ" and "Osiris". However, the "*ikr*", in the Pyramid Texts, has been identified with another quality. In PT 813, the king qualified himself, saying "I am more "*3ḫ*" than the "*3ḫw*", more "*ikr*" than the "*ikrw*", and more "*dd*" than "*ddw*". From the passage, we can understand that they were two different natures being quite distinguished out in meaning. In other words, the "*3ḫ*" implies a quite different significance from "*ikr*". On the other hand, "*ikr*" means "excellent and excellence" (Wb 1, 137.6).[338] The combination between "*3ḫ*" and "*ikr*" might mean "the beneficent soul"; in this case the "*3ḫ*" is that noun being qualified by the adjective "*ikr*". It can be considered merely as an epithet for the deceased one.[339] It qualifies the deceased one as having the power of being able to help his supporters and to act against his antagonists.[340] The dedicatee, as far as our knowledge extends, has

[336] Demarée 1983, 198.
[337] Assmann & Bommas 2002, 20-23.
[338] Kanawati & Abder-Raziq 1998, 47-49, pl. 24c, 64.
[339] Demarée 1983, 275.
[340] Ibid, 277.

not any particular distinction in the hierarchal society of Deir el-Medina. What is most distinct about this designation is that it gives us a dating clue, being confined from the XVIIIth down to the XXth dynasty.[341] Such expression can imply a new cultic tradition being highly culminated and stressed by the villagers of Deir el-Medina. It represents the so called "ancestors cult" which was practiced in the houses. Some scholars call this cult the "house-cult" which comprised "the adoration of some minor gods like Shed, Thueris, Renenutet and Meritseger" in and around Deir el-Medina village.[342]
[b] For "*Ḥrw*", it is hard to restore this proper name and to reassign it to a certain person. There are numerous personages bearing this name in the Village of Deir el-Medina.

Classification:
KVO 31 can not be ascribed to any sort of Valley of the Kings known accounts. It is clear that the ostracon was destined to be just a draft for a stela dedicated to its owner. Finding this stela amongst a royal predominant stuff may be out of place. We know that the Valley of the Kings is such a place where artisans constructed basically royal tombs along with their funerary stuff. We are wondering what a non-royal stuff has to do in the Valley of the Kings. Furthermore, were the workmen allowed to manufacture their own stuff in the Valley of the Kings? That can be answered by conducting a statistical process on the non-royal artefacts discovered in the Valley of the Kings. As far as our knowledge can save us, the stela manufacturing is found scarcely in the Valley of the Kings with respect to that of Deir el-Medina. Until 1983, there were found in Deir el-Medina 47 stelae designated with formula "*3ḫ iḳr n Rꜥ*"; only 6 were found in the Theban region.[343] Reeves has found, surprisingly, a votive stela with a scene of adoration before the serpent goddess "Meritseger" of the Theban mountain.[344] This stela was found under the natural checkpoint found beneath the modern tourists-path which runs between KV 11 of Ramses III and KV 57 of Horemoheb. In comparison to Deir el-Medina stela-drafts, we know that O. DeM 246 can be also classified as a draft for a stela as well. It contains a draft of the scribe *Pn-ṯ3-wr.t* adoring God Montu on it.[345] Unfortunately, such account is still in very scarce amount this is why we can not grasp a clear picture of it.

---

[341] Ibid, 281.
[342] Fitzenreiter 2008, 85-124.
[343] Demarée 1983, 279.
[344] www.nicholasreeves.com; Newsletter of the Valley of the Kings Foundation, No. 1 (2002), Nicholas Reeves (ed.). with contribution from Geoffery Martin, Stephen Quirke, Nicholas Reeves, Paul Sussman.
[345] McDowell 1999, 98, no. 70 (translation, commentary).

INTERPRETATION

The core of this research is 31 ostrca, 17 of which come from Davis's excavations in the Valley of the Kings. The rest (14) belongs to Carter/Carnavon's excavations. Before attempting to reassign the unprovenanced ostraca to more specific finding spots, we would like to get more insight into the history of these excavators and their endeavours in the Valley of the Kings.

Introduction to Davis excavations:
The early excavation seasons of Davis (1902 until 1904) were conducted by the Antiquities Services Inspector based in Luxor; H. Carter and J. E. Quibell were just assistants in those years. In 1905, Davis has relegated the new inspector A. Weigall to a supervisory role and brought forward E. R. Ayrton to be his assistant. Ayrton was succeeded by E. H. Jones who died in 1911 and then his place was occupied by H. Burton who continued working until the death of Davis year 1915. His published excavation accounts were not at the same level of the great discoveries he unveiled in the Valley of the Kings. Despite this fact, fortunately in the archive of the EES, there was discovered recently a series of the excavations' photos relating to years 1905/06, 07, 08. In addition to this, there was also found the day journal by Jones in the Egyptian Department of the Metropolitan Museum of Art along with some Photographs recently presented to Carmarthen Museum. The groundbreaking find is that there was found the sketch map locating the areas cleared and the site designations employed by Ayrton in year 1905/ 06. Davis's assistant (Ayrton) had given sites codes in ink or pencil to those ascertainable items found in those seasons. That has helped a mass of items, especially ostraca, to be reassigned to specific archaeological sites. Since the corpus of our ostraca come from the Valley of the Kings, we would like to define the locations of Davis's discoveries; exclusively those where ostraca were found, in the course of his excavations from years 1902 to 1914.
Findspots of ostraca found by Davis between years 1902-1914:

- Davis excavations year 1902: what follows is a group of ostraca published by Černy, ostraca, O. Cairo CG (1) 25576, (2) 25577, B. N (2) 25547, (7) 25744, (10) 25560, (18) (25553, 25636, 25672), and (37) 25642. These ostraca were found in different sites;
    - Site 3: the valley running from the main valley, beginning in front of KV 4 (Ramses XI) until KV 21 and beyond; at the end of the valley near KV 28 (anonymous) they found few ostraca;
    - Site 4: over the tomb of the prince "*M3-ḥr-p3-r*ᶜ", there were found many ostraca and small fragments of the XIX-XXth dynasty.[346]
- Davis excavations year 1903 (early January- 15 April): the small valley east of Seti I tomb, containing KV 19 and KV 20:
    - Site 6: in the entrance of KV 19 of (Ment-hi-khopshef) they found many hieratic ostraca.
- Davis excavations year 1905/06: numerous ostraca found in different locations and published by Černy, ostraca Cairo. The sites are (KV 2 of Ramses IV, KV13 of Bay, KV 14 of Tausert/ Setnakhte, KV 29 [anonymous], 35 of Amenophis II, and KV 53 [anonymous]). It is noteworthy mentioning that the bulk of the ostraca published in the Catalogue of ostraca of Cairo comes from KV 47 (Siptah);[347]
    - Site 13: in front of KV 2 of Ramses IV, there were found a series of ostraca and a hieratic ostracon, mentioning king Amenophis I;[348]
    - Site 14: in the northern face of the promontory which runs out from the perpendicular cliffs slightly south of the tomb of Amenophis II, they found one or two ostraca of dynasty XXth;[349]

---

[346] Carter 1903, 46.
[347] Reeves 1984, 227-235.
[348] Davis 1908, 6.
[349] Ibid, 7.

- Site 15: in 1905, discovery and partial clearance of KV 47. There were discovered three potsherds and ostraca with name of Seti II together with O. Cairo GC 25766 published by Černy, ostraca Cairo;[350]
- Site 16: the discovery of KV 49 (anonymous) where they found an ostracon with the name of the chief workmen "*Ḥ3y*";[351] slightly to the north of tomb KV 29 (anonymous), they discovered several ostraca; over the mouth of the same tomb they discovered remains of rough workmen's huts together with several ostraca;[352]
- Site 17: in 1906, in the entrance of KV 19 of (Ment-hi-Khopshef) they discovered several ostraca.

- Davis excavations 1906/07: a place about forty feet oblong in the vicinity of KV 55 of Queen Tiyi: they found a number of ostraca published in the Catalogue of Černy, ostraca Cairo.[353]
- Davis excavations 1907/08: they discovered a number of ostraca published in Catalogue Černy, Cairo coming from the area between KV 17 of Seti I-KV 21 (anonymous) which has workmen's houses;[354]
  - Site 19: between KV 18 and KV 21 there were some finds including ostraca;
  - Site 21, from the vicinity of KV 9 of Ramses V/VI they found some ostraca; continuation of work southwards along the path near KV 61 (anonymous) they found ostraca as well.[355]
- Davis excavations year 1908/09: between KV 57 (Hormoheb) and KV 35 (Amenophis II):
  - Site 23: they discovered two ostraca and two inscribed potsherds in debris opposite and in front of Hormoheb's tomb about 4 meters from the step;[356]
  - Site 25: they discovered several ostraca over the whole field and one limestone ostracon in the trench 1 meter deep all along the Wadi going through the path and shed.[357]
- Davis excavations year 1909/ 10: some 20- 30 m S of KV 50-52 (both anonymous), removing debris over the cliff from the monkey tomb:[358]
  - Site 28: to N and S along the footpath due E of KV 47 of Siptah, they found there several ostraca; a broken pot ostraca with the name of Ramses II;
  - Site 32: Clearance of sloping desert of all sides (presumably of KV 43 of Thutmosis IV and KV 20 of Hatshepsut) where they found several ostraca.

Introduction to Carter/ Carnarvon's excavations:

Davis died in February 1915 and after his death the concession of work at the royal tombs was passed to the Earl Fifth Carnarvon who was under the supervision of H. Carter. Their work results did not satisfy a number of excavators with exception of KV 62 of Tutankhamun. Nevertheless, full excavation records were properly done and to reconstruct their schemes of work, it does not require great effort. The ostraca in our corpus being assigned to their excavations are easily restored in terms of exact finding spot and year. Apart from their wide excavation spread in the Valley of the Kings and their discoveries to a new number of tombs, they had aimed to take on the former uncompleted excavations of Davis and clear up the debris hills accumulated by his former digging works.

Apart from the finding of ostraca, in the course of Davis/ Carter's excavations, there had been discovered a considerable number of huts spread throughout the Valley of the Kings and its lateral valleys. Most of scholars agree about the use of these huts as merely temporary stations for workers on the nine weekly days. In Amenmesse project, they have discovered recently in 2001 and 2003 two groups of houses for workmen, being divided on the east and the west sides of KV 10 (Amenmesse). They have named them (East and West Huts). In the East Huts, they found some ceramic and a few

---

[350] Ibid, 1.
[351] Daressy1922, 75-76.
[352] Reeves 1990, 305.
[353] Ibid, 307.
[354] Davis 1912, 262.
[355] Reeves 1990, 308.
[356] Ibid, 310.
[357] Ibid, 311-313.
[358] Ibid, 314.

ostraca. Surprisingly, none of the discoveries can assign to the king Amenmesse.[359] These huts may probably have served as mini-workshops/ settlements to execute the work of a certain king or some kings whose tombs are located in the vicinity.

In view of the activities of the Project ARTP (UK) in the Valley of the Kings, they have discovered a wide range of huts running from south to north and from east to west along with some spread throughout the lateral valleys.[360] The locations of these workshops/ settlements don't necessitate that there should exist items of the king whose tomb is in the vicinity. Therefore, the aim of this research is to handle out this point of argument and bring forward further debating issues as it is what our project is concerned about. Before getting into detail regarding our corpus of ostraca, we would like to relocate in a form of mapping charter, the finds of ostraca along with the workmen's huts found so far in the Valley of the Kings.

---

[359] Available on www.kv-10.com.

[360] Available on www.nicloasreeves.com.

Main findspots of ostraca discovered so far in the Valley of the Kings

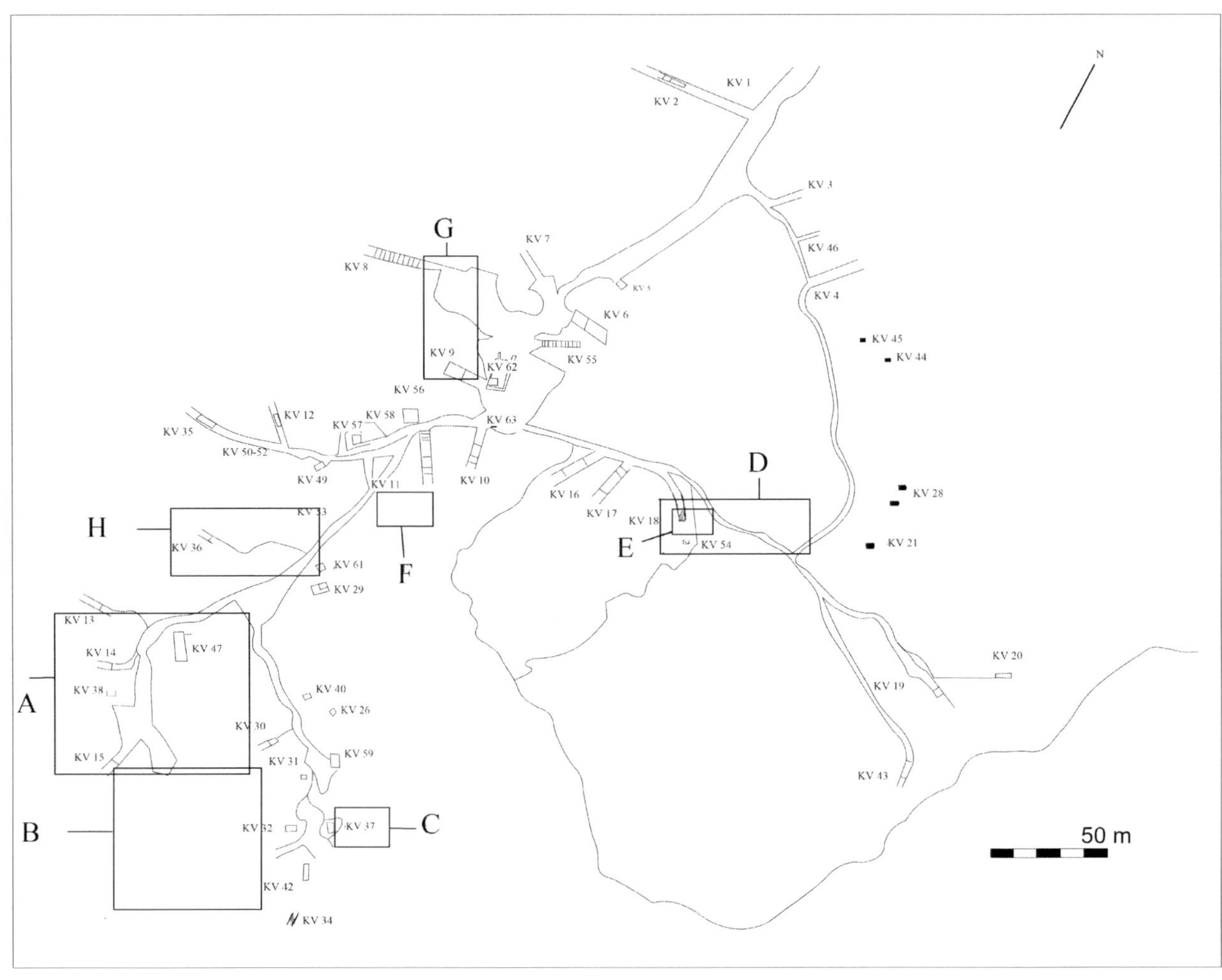

(A) Ostraca discovered by Davis, Carnarvon/Carter and MISR project of the end of the XIXth dynasty: main findspot is KV 47
(B) Ostraca discovered by Davis
(C) Ostraca discovered by Daressy
(D) Ostraca discovered by Davis
(E) Ostraca discovered by Davis and MISR project of the Ramesside Period (Ramses IV to Ramses VI): main findspost is KV 18
(F) Ostraca discovered by Davis
(G) Ostraca discovered by Carnarvon/Carter
(H) Ostraca discovered by the Service des Antiquités d'Egypte of the XIX-XXth dynasty

Provenance of the ostraca at the Metropolitan Museum of Art (New York)
Excavations Th. Davis 1907-1908 as recorded in the MMA Registers, provided by A. Oppenheim
(assistant curator in the Metropolitan Museum of Art)

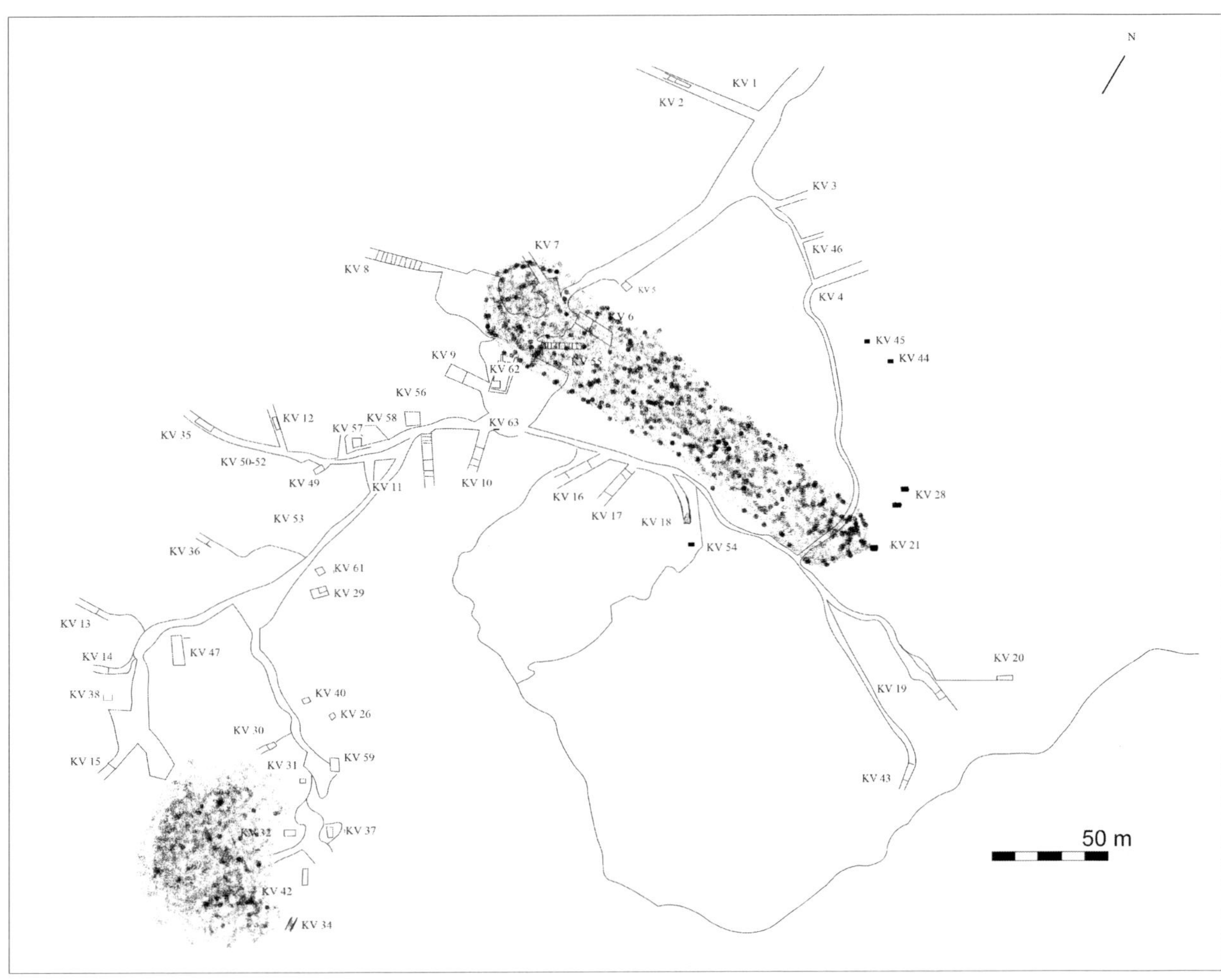

- A very wide and not well defined area between KV 8 (Merenptah) and KV 21
- On the right of the workmen's huts near Tiy tomb (KV 32)
- From the chip heaps in the same branch of the valley[361]

[361] I am deeply thankful to the assistant curator of the Metropolitan Museum of Art A. Opennheim who has provided me with this crucial data about Davis's excavations in excavation season 1907/08.

Map of the workmen's huts discovered so far in the Valley of the Kings

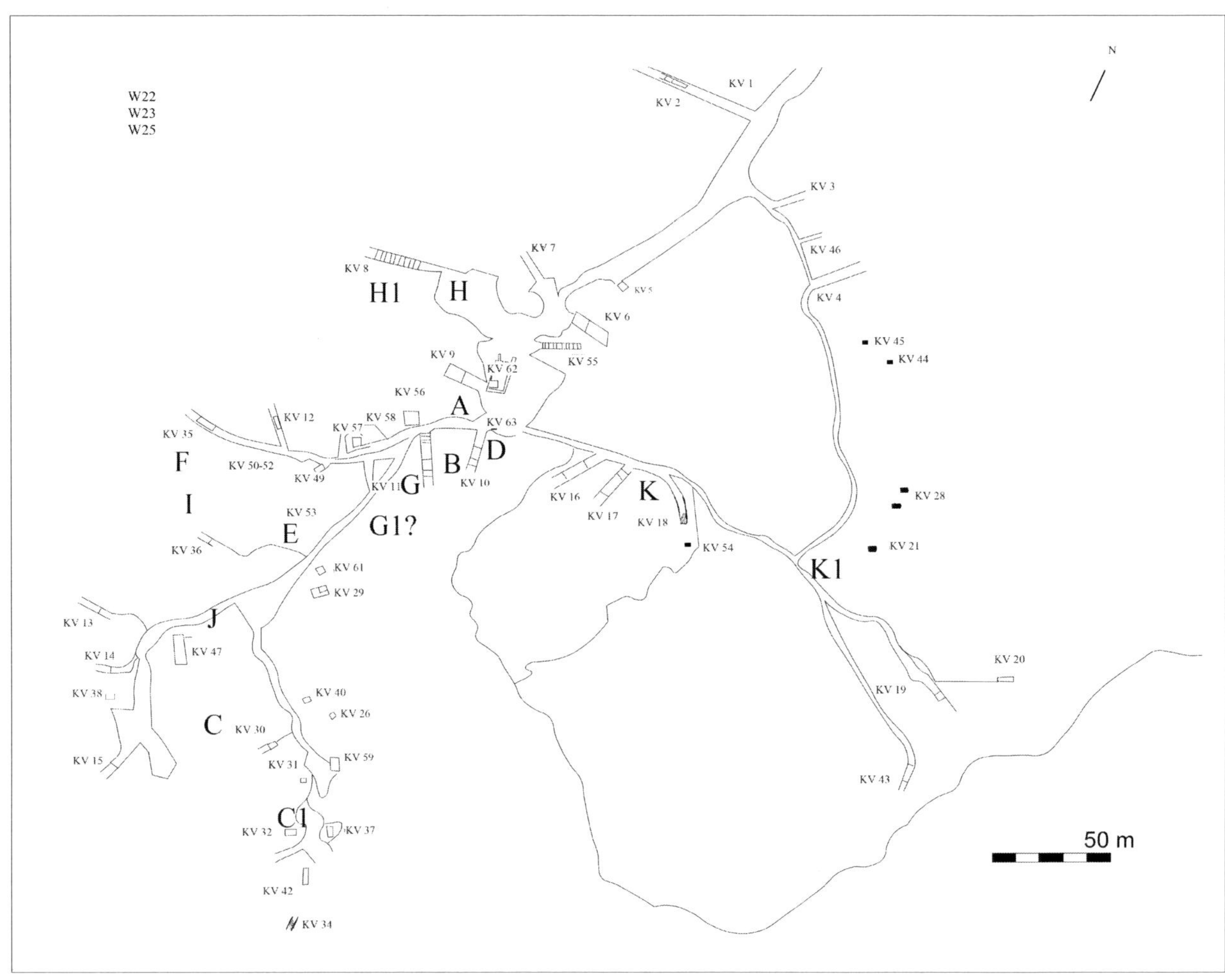

A between KV 9 (Ramses VI) and KV 56 (Gold Tomb) discovered by H. Carter and further investigated by Reeves: XXth dynasty

B between KV 10 (Amenmesse) and KV 11 (Ramses III) investigated by the Amarna Royal Tombs Project (UK)

C between KV 37 and KV 47 (Siptah) discovered by E. Ayrton on behalf of Th. Davis in 1905 and further investigated by the Amarna Royal Tombs Project (UK): Ramesside

C1 near KV 32 (Tiy)

D to the East of KV 10 (Amenmesse) investigated by the Amenmesse Project (Colorado, USA)

E over the mouth of KV 53

F to the South of KV 50-52

G to the South of KV 11 investigated by E. Ayrton on behalf of Th. Davis

G1? probable hut labelled KV 0 between KV 11 and KV 61

H valley leading to KV 8 (Merenptah) discovered by H. Carter

H1 south of KV 8 discovered by H. Carter

I region of KV 36 (Maiherperi)

J junction of the track leading to KV 47 (Siptah)

K South and South-East of Ramses X (KV 18) discovered by E. Ayrton on behalf of Th. Davis (season 1907-1908) and further investigated by MISR Project (Basel University, CH): Ramses IV-Ramses VI

K1 near KV 21 discovered by E. Ayrton on behalf of Th. Davis (season 1907-1908)

From the three maps, we can observe that there could be a relationship between the spread of the workmen's huts and the finding of ostraca in the Valley of the Kings. We may hypothesise that these workmen's huts might probably have been used as administrative stations where workmen could probably live in and craftily produce what should have been, then, transferred into royal tombs.
The majority of the ostraca published in Daressy's catalogue come from the clearance of royal tombs at the Valley of the Kings. That can be described as what follows:

- KV 18 (Ramses X) cleared in 1890
- KV 9 (Ramses VI) cleared in 1890. The ostraca coming from these two tombs were mixed up during the transport to Cairo so the scholar could not identify the exact provenance.
- KV 11 (Ramses III) cleared in 1892: O. Cairo CG 25008, 25013
- KV 37 (anonymous), wadi cleared in 1899: O. Cairo GC 25020-25023, 25055, 25069, 25973, 25081, 25089, 25104, 25112, 25127, 25178-25180, 25189bis, 25228, 25248-25249, 25269, 25293, 25297-25398, 25313-25315, 25321, 25352, 25354, 25357, 25360, 25362, 25364

Černy's catalogue includes documents from different provenances, but the bulk comes from the Valley of the Kings:

- Clearance of the tombs by Daressy: O. Cairo CG 25626, 25628, 25629
- Excavations of Davis subdivided as follows:
    - Not attributable to a precise season: "beneath G α.9": O. Cairo GC 25657
      "β": O. Cairo GC 25648
      "EQ": O. Cairo GC 25599, O. Cairo CG 25634
      "Q": O. Cairo GC 25571
    - Season 1902
    - Season 1905-1906
    - Season1906-1907
    - Season 1907-1908
    - Season 1908-1909
- Excavations Carnarvon/Carter as follows:
    - Season 1917-1918
    - Season 1922

As a matter of fact, we can also realize that the bulk of the ostraca published and assigned to the latter half of the XIXth dynasty in Cairo Museum, comes from four basic sites (KV 47 of Siptah has the major part of those ostraca, KV 13 of Bay, KV 14 Tauesert, and KV 15 Seti II).[362] The entry of the ostraca into Cairo Museum, we are concerned about in this project, had occurred at the same time of those already published in the Catalogue of Černy. In addition, the major part of the ostraca

[362] Černy 1935a, passim; Daressy 1901, *passim*.

unpublished in Cairo Museum, including my corpus had been seen and briefly commented in the Inventory Registers by Černy. He had most probably left them out for future work as they probably did not hold any vivid auxiliary elements for dating at that time. Accordingly, we will be relying on the dating framework of each ostracon as an essential tool to help us set out probable locations for those ostraca left without defined findspots.

KVO 2 has some marks on the *verso* which could be classified as "Funny-sings". There is also another mark "BM" along with a circle drawn in which there is number "5". If this number corresponds to a tomb, most probably the reference may be to "site 2" of the excavations conducted by Davis/Carter in 1902, in the Valley of the Kings.[363] Then, we could probably assign the finding spot to the area between KV5 and the opposite side of KV3, including the debris of KV5.[364]

As regards KVO 6, we may be able to draw up more assertive conclusions as it is mentioned in the Inventory Register that the ostracon was found in year 1905/06 of Davis's excavations. Based on the Davis' excavations in that season, we have seen that in site 15, in year 1905, the first discovery of KV 47 was triggered off and there had been done a partial clearance to the same tomb. In the course of clearance, they had found three potsherds and ostraca with Seti II's name. Together with these ostraca there was found also O. Cairo CG 25766 which is published in the catalogue of Cairo Museum of the ostraca.[365] Černy suggests that even this ostracon may attribute to the end of the XIXth dynasty according to its palaeography. That implies that KVO 6 might have been amongst these ostraca. Interesting enough is that KVO 6 is marked on its back with "X_2", like O. Cairo CG 25521 (year 1 and 2 of Siptah) whose fragments are marked with "X_1, X_{22}, X_{41}". Looking up in the sketch map of Ayrton, the site "X" can be located north-east of KV 13 (Bay) and downwards the tomb of "*Mꜥ-ḥr-pꜣ-rꜥ*".[366] We are wondering whether the designated capitalized letter "X" corresponds to the place where KVO 6 was found. If so, then KVO 6 may assign as a findspot to north-east of KV 13.

KVO 13 refers to an enclosure by mentioning the word "*inb*". We are wondering what kind of enclosure the scribe wanted to indicate to. The recent find of Reeves of a shrine and cross-wall running deeply beneath the modern tourist-path between KV57 (Horemheb) and KV11 (Ramses III) confirms the existence of a certain wall.[367] There was found also a limestone bluff, swinging round at the north to give restricted access to the valley. It was a natural checkpoint during the Ramesside Period protected by guards whose water-jars and hearth were uncovered as well. Furthermore, they found also some relieves in the wall of the rock-cut shrine. Some god figures were found also of Atum, Isis, and Meretseger along with undisturbed votive-stela for over thirty centuries. We wonder whether this wall can correspond to the same "*inb*" being mentioned in this ostracon. Even if it was the same wall, we can not venture on attributing KVO 13 to the same site where this wall was found although we can not rule out this probability completely.

KVO 14 was designated Carnarvon/ 285. It was found in the excavations conducted by Carter/Carnarvon in 1920- Spring 1921 (1 December-3/ 13 March). The main target of these excavations was to clear the rubbish mounds accumulated by the former excavations of Davis. Basic sources are Carter. MSS, I. J. 386-7, nos 276- 350. The site in which this ostracon was found is number 9 where the lateral valley between tombs Ramses II and VI' (KV 7- KV 9) runs.[368] This ostracon was there unearthed along with others published by Černy (278= O. Cairo CG 25788[369]; 279 = O. Cairo CG 25789[370]; 280 = O. Cairo CG 25823).

KVO 16 was found in the excavations conducted by Carter/ Carnarvon between Winter 1920-Spring 1921 (1 December-3/13 March).[371] The exact finding spot of this ostracon is "the nearby area

---

363 http://www.leidenuniv.nl/nino/dmd/dmd.html.

364 Reeves 1990, 293.

365 Černy 1935a, 82, pl. XCVIII.

366 Reeves 1990, 299- 300 (look it up in the sktech map of Ayrton year 1905/06).

367 http://www.nicholasreeves.com/artp.aspx?page=2.

368 Reeves 1990, 328.

369 Černy 1935b, 88, 111, pl CVI (description, transcription, facsimile) ; Helck 2002 , 87 (translation); KRI IV, 158 and 159 (transcription). This ostracon is dated by Helck to year 6 of Merenptah's reign.

370 Černy 1935b, 89, 111, pl CVI (description, transcription). The attribution of dating is to Amenmesse's reign (end of XIX Dynasty) by Helck 2002, 87; KRI IV 235.

371 Carter MSS, I.J.386-7, nos 276-350.

of the entrance of king Ramses VI's tomb (KV9) (23 December-?3 January) (Site H). The ostracon was designated "292" as excavation number.
One of the fragments of KVO 17 is designated Carnarvon/ 300. [372] According to the records of Carter/ Carnarvon, This fragment was found beside the entrance of KV 9 (Ramses VI). We suppose that the other fragments might have been discovered in the course of events of the former excavations of Davis and were not systematically recorded. When Černy looked over the ostraca of Cairo Museum could realize that these scattered pieces could have constituted one ostracon.
KVO 18 was discovered in the excavations conducted by H. Carter in Winter 1920- Spring 1921 (1 December- 03/13 March).[373] The sites excavated were designated H, I, L; attribution of finds by number. This ostracon is designated 301. The exact finding spot of this ostracon was beside the entrance of KV 9 of king Ramses VI.[374] This finding place was used to mix mortar or plaster and there were built huts partly upon ground made up with numbers of boulders.
KVO 19 was found in the excavations conducted by Carter/Carnarvon in 1922 (8 February- "March").[375] The attested site designation is "K". The site number in which this ostracon was found is "17": "recommended excavations on the east side of foot-hill containing the tomb of Siptah (KV47)". The ostracon was designated "371" and found among a group of other ostraca, bearing excavation numbers 367-78.
We have relied sometimes on the dating framework of several ostraca along with the information published by Reeves being extracted exactly from the day-journal records of Davis' assistant (Ayrton). We have actually profoundly checked out the ostraca published by Černy whose corpus was taken mostly from the excavations of Davis. This endeavour has established a vivid outline which helped us speculate on the location of some unprovenanced ostraca. The fact that there are many ostraca left out of the corpus without handling them with more detailed analysis with regard to their findspots is accounted for the lack of information these ostraca have. These unhandled ostraca might be better defined with the forthcoming publications of some missions in the Valley of the Kings; like MISR, Amenmesse, and ARTP project. We do believe that my ostraca can complement those discovered by these missions. Until they publish their material, the group of ostraca in question may remain away from the spot light.

---

[372] Reeves 1990 , 328.
[373] Carter, MSS, I. J. 386-7, nos 276-350.
[374] Reeves 1990, 328.
[375] Carter, MSS, I.J. 387, nos 351-432.

ABBREVIATIONS

ÄAT	Ägypten und Alten Testament
ASAE	Annales du services des antiquités égyptiennes
BdE	Bibliothèque d'Étude
BIFAO	Bulletin de l'Institut français d'archéologie
BMMA	Bulletin of the Metropolitan Museum of Arts
ChdE	Chronique d'Égypte
DFIFAO	Documents de fouilles de l'Institut français d'archéologie orientale
EA	Egyptian Archaeology
EU	Egyptologische uitgaven
IFAO	Institut français d'archéologie orientale
JARCE	Journal of the American Research Centre in Egypt
JEA	Journal of Egyptian Archaeology
JNES	Journal of Near Eastern Studies
JSSEA	Journal of the Society of the Studies of Egyptian Antiquities
MÄS	Münchener ägyptologische Studien
MIFAO	Memoires de l'Institut français d'archéologie orientale
MIO	Mitteilungen des Instituts für Orientforshung des deutschen Akademie der Wissenschaften zu Berlin
NINO	Nederlands Instituut voor het Nabije Oosten
OBO	Orbis Biblicus et Orientalis
OLA	Orientalia Lovaniensa Analecta
RdE	Revue d'Égyptologie
SAK	Studien zur ältägyptischen Kultur
ZÄS	Zeitschrift für ägyptische Sprache und Kunstgeschichte

BIBLIOGRAPHY

Adrom 2008 — F. Adrom, Katrin & A. Schülter, Altägyptische Weltsichten: Akten des Symposiums zur historischen Topographie und T oponymie Altägyptens vom 12.-14. Mai 2006 in München, ÄAT 68, Harrassowitz: Wiesbaden

Al-Ayedi 2006 — A. R. Al-Ayedi, Index of Egyptian administrative, religious and military titles of the New Kingdom, Obelisk Publications: Ismailia

Aling 1976 — A. Aling, Prosopographical Study of the Reigns of Thutmosis IV and Amenhotep III, PhD Dissertation University of Minnesota

Allam 1973 — S. Allam, Hieratische Ostraka und Papyri aus der Ramessidenzeit, Urkunden zum Rechtsleben im Alten Ägypten I, by the author: Tübingen

Allen 2000 — J. P. Allen, Middle Egyptian: An introduction to the language and culture of the hieroglyphs, Cambridge University Press: Cambridge

Allen 1949 — T. G. Allen, Some Egyptian Sun Hymns, JNES 8/4, 349-355

Andreu 2002 — G. Andreu ed., Les artistes de Pharaon. Deir el-Médineh et la Vallée des Rois, Editions de la Réunion des musées nationaux, Faton: Dijon

Armour 2001 — R.A. Armour, Gods and Myths of Ancient Egypt, The American University in Cairo Press: Cairo

Assmann 1999 — J. Assmann, Ägyptische Hymnen und Gebete: Übersetzt, kommentiert und eingeleitet, OBO, Univiversität Freiburg: Freiburg (Schweiz) and Göttingen

Assmann & Bommas 2002 — J. Assmann & M. Bommas, Altägyptische Totenliturgien/1: Totenliturgien in den Sargtexten des Mittleren Reiches Schriften der Heidelberg Akademie der Wissenschaften, Philosophisch-Historische Klasse Supplemente 14, Universitätsverlag C. Winter: Heidelberg

Baines & Malek 1980 — J. Baines & J. Malek Atlas of ancient Egypt, Phaidon: Oxford

Bakir 1983 — M.A. Bakir, Notes on Late Egyptian Grammar: A Semitic approach. An introduction to the study of the Egyptian Language, Aris & Phillips: Warminster

Barta1968 — W. Barta, Aufbau und Bedeutung der altägyptischen Opferformel, Agyptologische Forshungen 24, J. J. Augustin: Glückstadt and New York

Beckerath 1994 — J. Beckerath von, Papyrus Turin 1898+, Verso, SAK 21, 29- 33

Beckerath 1999 — J. Beckerath von, Handbuch der ägyptischen Königsnamen, MÄS 49, 2nd edition, Philip von Zabern: Mainz am Rhein

Bierbrier 1982 — M. L. Bierbreir et al., Notes de prosopographie thébaine. Deuxiéme série. The family of Amenemone at Deir El-Medina, CdhE 57, 201-230

Bierbrier 1982 — M. L. Bierbreir ed, Hieratic Texts from Egyptian Stelae Etc. Part X, the Trustees of the British Museum: London

Bogoslovsky 1980 — E. S. Bogoslovsky, Hundred Egyptian Draughtsmen, ZÄS 107, 89-116

Bogoslovsky 1981 — E. S. Bogoslovsky, On the system of the Ancient Egyptian Society of the Epoch of the New Kingdom. According to Documents from Deir el-Medina, Altorientalische Forschungen 8, 5-21

Bommas 2006 — M. Bommas, Ostrakon Zürich 1892. Eines der jüngsten Zeugnisse der Sinuhe-Erzählung aus dem Alten Ägypten, Archaeölogische Sammlung der Universität Zürich 32 (2006), 7-16.

Bouvoier 2003 — G. Bouvoeir, Catalogue des étiquettes de jarres hiératiques inédites de l'Institut d'Égyptologie de Strasbourg, DFIFAO 43, IFAO: Le Caire

Breasted 1907 — J. H. Breasted, Ancient records of Egypt: Historical Documents, from the Earliest Times to the Persian Conquest, collected, edited and translated with commentary, vol. V, The University of Chicago Press: Chicago

Brovarski 2001 — E. Brovarski, The Snedjemib Complex Part I. The Mastabas of Senedjemib Inti (G 2370), Khnumenti (G 2374), and Senedjemib Mehi (G 2378), Giza Mastabas 7, Museum of Fine Arts: Boston

Brunner-Traut 1989 — E. Brunner-Traut, Altägyptische Märchen. Mythen und andere volkstümliche Erzählungen, Eugen Diederichs: München

Bruyère 1928 — B. Bruyère, Rapport sur les fouilles de Deir el Médineh, FIFAO 6, IFAO: Le Caire

Bruyère 1952 — B. Bruyère, Rapport sur les fouilles de Deir el Médineh, 1935-1940, FIFAO 20, IFAO: Le Caire

Bruyère 1937b — B. Bruyère, Rapport sur les fouilles de Deir el Médineh, 1934-1935. Deuxième partie. La nécropole de l'Est, FIFAO 15, IFAO: Le Caire

Bruyère 1959 — B. Bruyère, La tombe N° 1 de Sen-Nedjem à Deir el-Medineh, MIFAO 88, IFAO: Le Caire

Caminos 1977 — R. A. Caminos, A Tale of Woe : From a Hieratic Papyrus in the A.S. Pushkin Museum of Fine Arts in Moscow, Griffith Inst./Ashmolean Museum: Oxford

Carter 1903 — M. H. Carter, Report on General Work done in the Southern Inspectorate, ASAE 4, 43-50

Černy 1929 — J. Černy, Papyrus Salt 124 (Brit. Mus. 10055), JEA 15, 243-258

Černy 1931 — J. Černy, Les ostraca hiératiques, leur intérêt et la nécessité de leur étude, ChdE VI/12 (1931), 212-224

Černy 1935a — J. Černy, Catalogue des ostraca hiératiques non littéraires de Deir el Médineh. Tome I. Nos 1 à 339, DFIFAO 3, IFAO: Le Caire

Černy 1935b — J. Černy, Catalogue général des antiquités égyptiennes du Musée du Caire (Nr. 25501-25832): ostraca hiératiques, Service des Antiquités de l'Égypte, IFAO: Le Caire

Černy 1939a — J. Černy, Catalogue des ostraca hiératiques non littéraires de Deir el Médineh. Tome IV. Nos 242 à 339, DFIFAO 6, IFAO: Le Caire

Černy 1939b — J. Černy, Late Ramesside Letters, Bibliotheca aegyptiaca 9, Bruxelles

Černy 1965 — J. Černy, Hieratic Inscriptions from the Tomb of Tutankhamun, Tutankhamun's Tomb Series 2, Griffith Institute: Oxford

Černy 2004 — J. Černy J, A community of workmen at Thebes in the Ramesside Period, BdE 50 3rd edtion, IFAO: Le Caire

Černy & Gardiner 1957 — J. Černy & A. H. Gardiner, Hieratic Ostraca, Griffith Institute: Oxford

Černy & Israelit Groll 1984 — J. Černy & S. Israelit Groll, A Late Egyptian Grammar, 3rd updated edition, Ed. Pontificio Istituto Biblico: Rome

Černy & Sadek 1970 — J. Černy & A. A. Sadek, Graffiti de la montagne Thébaine IV. Transcription et indices, CEDAE: Le Caire

Champollion 1835-1845 — J.-F. Champollion, Monuments de l'Égypte et de la Nubie: D'après les dessins exécutés sur les lieux sous la dir. de Champollion le-Jeune et les descriptions autographes qu'il en a rédigées, vols I-II, Didot: Paris

Chirstophe 1951 — L.-A. Chirstophe, La carrier du prince Merenptah et les trios régences ramessides, ASAE 51, 335-372

Collier 1985 — M. Collier, Papyrus BM 10052 3,17, Wepwawet research papers in Egyptology 1, 5-6.

Collier 2004 — M. Collier, Dating Late XIXth Dynasty Ostraca, EU 18, NINO: Leiden

Collier & Quirke 2004 — M. Collier & S. Quirke, The UCL Lahun Papyri: Religious, literary, legal, mathematical and medical, BAR International Series 1110, Archaeopress: Oxford

Daressy 1901 — G. E. J. Daressy, Catalogue général des Antiquités Égyptiennes du Musée du Caire (Nos 25001-25383): Ostraca, catalogue général des Antiquités Égyptiennes 1, IFAO: Le Caire

Daressy 1922 — G. E. J. Daressy, Un ostracon de Biban el Molouk, ASAE 22, 75-76

Daressy 1927 — G. E. J. Daressy, Quelques ostraca de Biban el-Molouk, ASAE 27, 161-182

Davies 1997 — B. G. Davies, Egyptian Historical Inscriptions of the Nineteenth Dynasty, Aegyptiaca 2, Paul Åströms förlag: Jonsered

Davies 1999 — B. G. Davies, Who is who at Deir El- Medina: A prosopographic study of the royal workmen's community, EU 13, NINO: Leiden

Davies 1902 — N. de G. Davies, The Rock tombs of Deir El Gebrâwi. Part II. Tomb of Zau and Tombs of the Northern Group, Archaeological Survey of Egypt Memoir 12, Egypt Exploration Fund: London

Davis 1908 — T. M. Davis, The Tomb of Siptah: The Monkey Tomb and the Gold Tomb: The Discovery of the Tombs; illustrations in color by E. Harold Jones. King Siptah and Queen Tauosîrt/ by Gaston Maspero. The excavations of 1905-1907/ by Edward Ayrton. Catalogue of the objects discovered/ by G. Daressy

Constable: London
Davis 1912 T. M. Davis, The tombs of Harmhabi and Toutânkhamoun: The discovery of the tombs. King Harmhabi and Toutânkhamoun/ by Sir Gaston Maspero. Catalogue of the objects discovered/ by G. Daressy, Duckworth: London
Demarée 1983 R. J. Demarée, The "3h iḳr n Rc" stelae. On ancestor worship in ancient Egpyt, EU 3, NINO: Leiden
Demarée 2002 R. J. Demarée, Ramesside Ostraca, The British Museum Press: London
Demarée 2006 R. J. Demarée, The Bankes Late Ramesside Papyri, British Museum Research Publications 155, British Museum: London
Donker van Heel & Haring 2003 K. Donker van Heel & B. J. J. Haring, Writing in Workmen's Village: Scribal Practice in Ramesside Deri el-Medina, EU 16, NINO: Leiden
Dorn 2004 A. Dorn, Die Lehre Amunnachts, ZÄS 131, 38-55
Engelbach 1930 R. Engelbach, Monuments of Prince Merenptah from Athribis (Benha), ASAE 30, 197-202
Erichsen 1933 W. Erichsen, Papyrus Harris I, Bibliotheca Aegyptiaca V, Fondation Égyptologique Reine Élisabeth: Bruxelles
Fisher 2001 M.M. Fisher, The Sons of Ramesses II, ÄAT 53/1-2, Harrassowitz: Wiesbaden
Fitzenreiter 2008 M. Fitzenreiter, *ꜣḫ n jtn ꜥḥꜣ ꜣḫ jḳr n Rꜥ*: Die königlichen Familienstelen und die religiöse Praxis in Amarna, SAK 37, 85-124
Gaballa 1977 G. A. Gaballa, The Memphite Tomb-Chapel of Mose, Aris & Phillips: Warminster
Gardiner 1911 A. H. Gardiner, Egyptian Hieratic Texts: Transcribed, translated and annotated. Series. Literary Texts of the New Kingdom. The Papyrus Anastasi I and the Papyrus Koller together with the Parallel Texts, J. C. Hinrichs'sche Buchhandlung: Leipzig
Gardiner 1923 A.H. Gardiner, The Eloquent Peasant, JEA 9, 5-25
Gardiner 1932 A. H. Gardiner, Late Egyptian stories, Bibliotheca Aegyptiaca 1, Fondation Égyptologique Reine Élisabeth: Bruxelles
Gardiner 1937 A. H. Gardiner, Late Egyptian Miscellanies, Bibliotheca Aegyptiaca 7, Fondation Égyptologique Reine Élisabeth: Bruxelles
Gardiner 1947 A.H. Gardiner, Acient Egyptian Onomastica, Oxford University Press: London
Gardiner 1948 G. Gardiner, The Founding of a New Delta Town in the Twentieth Dynasty, JEA 34, 19-22.
Gasse 2005 A. Gasse, Catalogue des ostraca littéraires de Deir el-Médîna. Tome V. Nos 175-1873 et 1156, DFIFAO 44, IFAO: Le Caire
Gauthier 1914 H. Gauthier, Le livre des rois d'Égypte III, MIFAO 19, IFAO: Le Caire
Goedicke 1968 H. Goedicke, Remarks on the Hymns to Sesostris III, JARCE 7, 23-26
Gomaà 1973 F. Gomaà, Chaemwese Sohn Ramses' II, und Hoberpriester von Memphis, ÄAT 27, Harrasowitz: Wiesbaden

Goyon 1972 — J.-C. Goyon, Confirmation du pouvoir royal au nouvel an (Brooklyn Museum Papyrus 47.218.50), BdE 52, IFAO: Le Caire

Goyon 1999 — J.-C. Goyon, Le papyrus d'Imouthès, fils de Psintaês, au Metropolitan Museum of Art de New York (Papyrus MMA 35.9.21), The Metropolitan Museum of Art: New York

Grandet 2000 — P. Grandet, Catalogue des ostraca hiératiques non littéraires de Deir el-Médinéh/8: Nos 706-830, DFIFAO 39, IFAO: Le Caire

Grandet 2003 — P. Grandet, Travaux grèves et personnages célèbres aux XIXe et XXe dynasties, dans quelques ostraca documentaires de l'IFAO, in G. Andreu ed., Deir el-Médineh et la Vallée des Roi: La vie en Égypte au temps des pharaons du Nouvel Empire. Actes du colloque organisé par le musée du Louvre les 3 et 4 mai 2002, Éditions Khéops: Paris, 209-233

Grandet 2003 — P. Grandet, Catalogue des ostraca hiératiques non littéraires de Deir el-Médinéh/9: Nos 831 – 1000, DFIFAO 41, IFAO : Le Caire

Grandet 2006 — P. Grandet, Catalogue des ostraca hiératiques non littéraires de Deir el-Médinéh/10: nos 10001 – 10123, DFIFAO 46, IFAO: Le Caire

Grapow 1953 — H. Grapow, Liederkranz zu ehren Königs Sesostris des dritten aus Kahun, MIO 1, 189-209

Häggman 2002 — S. Häggman, Directing Deir el-Medina: The External Administration of the Nercropolis, Uppsala Studies in Egyptology 4, Department of Archaeology and Ancient History Uppsala University: Uppsala

Haring 1997 — J.J. Ben Haring, Divine Households: Adminstartive and economic aspects of the New Kingdom Royal memorial temples in western Thebes, EU 12, NINO: Leiden

Hayes 1951 — W. C. Hayes, Inscriptions from the Palace of Amenhotep III, JNES 10 35-56, 82-111, 156-83, 231-42.

Helck 1959 — W. Helck, Bemerkungen zu den Thronbesteigungsdaten im Neuen Reich, Studia biblica et orientalia. Volume III: Oriens antiquus Roma, 113-129 = Analecta biblica 12, 113-129

Helck 1963 — W. Helck, Materialien zur Wirtschaftsgeschichte des Neuen Reiches: Eigentum und Besitz an verschiedenen Dingen des täglichen Lebens Kapitel, vol. III, Steiner: Wiesbaden

Helck 1965 — W. Helck, Materialien zur Wirtschaftsgeschichte des Neuen Reiches: Eigentum und Besitz an verschiedenen Dingen des täglichen Lebens Kapitel, vol. V, Steiner: Wiesbaden

Helck 2002 — W. Helck, Die Datierten und datierbaren Ostraka: Papyri und Graffiti von Deir el-Medineh (bearbeitet von Adelheid Schlott), Harrasowitz: Wiesbaden

Hornung 1991 — E. Hornung, The Tomb of Pharaoh Seti I: Das grab Sethos' I, Artemis Verlag: München and Zürich

Hornung & Stähelin 2006 — E. Hornung & E. Stähelin, Neue studien zum Sedfest,

Ägyptiaca Helvetica 20, Schwabe Verlag: Basel

Hourig 1989 — S. Hourig, Les monuments du roi Merenptah, Sonderschrift des deutschen archäologisches Instituts. Abteilung Kairo 22, Philipp von Zabern: Mainz am Rhein

Janssen 1975 — J. J. Janssen, Commodity Prices from the Ramesside Period: an Economic Study of the Village of Necropolis Workmen at Thebes, E. J. Brill: Leiden

Janssen 1982 — J.J. Janssen, Two Personalities, in R. J. Demarée ed., Gleanings from Deir el-Medîna, EU 1, NINO: Leiden, 109-131

Janssen 1991 — J. J. Janssen, Late Ramesside Letters and Communications, Hieratic Papyri in the British Museum 6, British Museum Press: London

Janssen 1992 — J. J. Janssen, Gear for the Tombs, RdE 43, 107-122

Janssen 2005 — J. J. Janssen, Donkeys at Deir el-Medina, EU 19, NINO: Leiden

Jauhiainen 2009 — H. Jauhiainen, Do not celebrate your feast without your neighbours : a study of references to feasts and festivals in non-literary documents from Ramesside period Deir el Medina, Publications of the Institute for Asian and African Studies 10, Helsinki University Print: Helsinki

Johnson 1986 — J. Johnson, Thus Wrote 'Onchsheshonqy. An Introductory Grammar of Demotic, Studies in the Ancient Oriental Civilization 45, Oriental Institute of the University of Chicago: Chigago (Ill.)

Jones 2000 — D. Jones, An Index of Ancient Egyptian Titles, Epithets and Phrases of the Old Kingdom, 2 vols., BAR International Series 866, Archaeopress: Oxford

Kanawati 1986 — N. Kanawasti, The rock tombs of El-Hawawish:The Cemetery of Akhmim vol. 6, Macquire Ancient History Association: Sydney

Kanawati & Abder-Raziq 1998 — N. Kanawati & M. Abder-Raziq, The Teti Cemetery at Saqqara III: the Tombs of Neferseshemre and Seankhuiptah, American Centre for Egyptology Reports 11, Aris & Phillips: Warminster

Kanawati 2002 — N. Kanawati, Tombs at Giza. II: Seshathetep/Heti (G5150), Nesutnefer (G4970) and Seshemnefer II (G5080), Australian Centre for Egyptology Reports 18, Warminster 2002

KRI — Kitchen 1975-1990 K. Kitchen, Ramesside Inscription: Historical and Biographical , 8 vols., B. H. Blackwell: Oxford

KRI translation — Kitchen 1993- K. Kitchen, Ramesside Inscription. Translated and Annoted, B.H. Blackwell: Oxford

Lalouette 1987 — C. Lalouette, Textes sacrés et textes profanes de l'ancienne Égypte, vol 2 : Mythes, contes et poésies, Gallimard : Paris

Lapp 1997 — G. Lapp, The Papyrus of Nu (BM EA 10477) Catalogue of the Books of the Dead in the British Museum 1, British Museum Press: London

Lasing 1918 — A. Lansing, The Egyptian expedition 1916-17: Excavations at the palace of Amenhotep III at Thebes, BMMA 13, 8-14

Leahy 1978 — M. A. Leahy, The inscriptions, D. O'Connor & B. J. Kemp, Excavations at Malqata and the Birket Habu 1971-1974, Egyptology Today vol. 4, Aris & Phillips: Warminster

Lesko & Lesko 1982-1990 — L. H. Lesko & B. Lesko, A dictionary of Late Egyptian, 5 vols, B. C. Scribe Publ.: Berkeley (Calif.)

López 1978-1984 — J. López, Ostraca ieratici Catalogo del Museo Egizio di Torino. Serie Seconda. Collezioni vol. 3 fasc. 1-4, Istituto editoriale cisalpino, la Goliardica: Milano

Lüddeckens 1994 — E. Lüddeckens ed., Aegyptische Handschriften, Verzeichnis der orientalischen Handschriften in Deutschland 19/4 beschriben von G. Burkard & H. Fischer-Elfert, Franz Steiner: Wiesbaden and Stuttgart

McDowell 1993 — A. G. McDowell, Hieratic Ostraca in the Hunterian Museum Glasgow (the Colin Campbell Ostraca), Griffith Institute/Ashmonlean Museum: Oxford

McDowell 1995 — A. G. McDowell, An Inscribed Hieratic Ostracon (Ashmolean HO 655), JEA 81, 220-225

McDowell 1999 — A. G. McDowell, Village Life in Ancient Egypt: Laundry Lists and Love Songs, Oxford University Press: Oxford

McGovern 1997 — P. E. McGovern, Wine of Egypt's Golden Age: an Archaeochemical Perspective, JEA 83, 69-108

Meeks 1978 — D. Meeks, Année lexicographique/2, Meeks : Paris

Meeks 1979 — D. Meeks, Année lexicographique/3, Meeks : Paris

Möller 1927 — G. Möller, Hieratische Paläographie: die ägyptische Buchschrift in ihrer Entwicklung von der 5. Dynastie bis zur römischen Kaiserzeit, Bd. II : von der zeit Thutmosis' III bis zum Ende der einundzwanzigsten Dynastie, Hinrichs: Leipzig

Neveu 1998 — F. Neveu, La langue des Ramsès: grammaire du néo-égyptien, Khéops : Paris

Ogdon 1978-1979 — J. R. Ogdon, The Old Kingdom Name for the Canopic Branch of the Delta, JSSEA 9, 65-74

Peet 1930 — T. E. Peet, The Great Tomb-Robberies of the Twentieth Egyptian Dynasty, 2 vols, Clarendon Press: Oxford

Peust 1999 — C. Peust, Egyptian Phonology: an Introduction to the Phonology of a Dead Language, Monographien zur ägyptischen Sprache 2, Peust & Gutschmidt: Göttingen

Piankoff 1941 — A. Piankoff, Le livre des Quererts. 1er Tableau, BIFAO 41, 1-11

PM — Porter & Moss 1927- B. Porter & R. Moss, Topographical Bibliography of ancient Egyptian hieroglyphic texts, reliefs, and paintings, vols 1-5, Clarendon Press Griffith Institute: Oxford

Pomorska 1987 — I. Pomorska, Les flabellifères à la droite du roi en Égypte ancienne, Éditions scientifiques de Pologne : Varsovie

Posener 1934-1980 — G. Posener, Catalogue des ostraca hiératiques littéraires de Deir el-Médineh. Nos 1001 à 1675, DFIFAO 18/1-3 IFAO: Le Caire

Posener 1955 — G. Posener, L'exorde de l'instruction éducative d'Amennakhte, RdE 10 (1955), 61-72

Quack 2004 — J. F. Quack, Der pränatale Geschlechtsverkehr von Isis und Osiris sowie eine Notiz zum Alter des Osiris, SAK 32, 327-332

RAD — A. H. Gardiner, Ramesside administrative documents, Oxford University Press: London 1948

Radwan 1987 — A. Radwan, Six Ramesside Stelae in the Popular Pyramidion-Form, ASAE 71, 223-228

RPN — Ranke 1935-1977 H. Ranke, Die ägyptischen Personennamen, vols I-III, Augustin: Glückstadt

Reeves 1984 — C. N. Reeves, Excavations in the Valley of the Kings, 1905/6: a Photographic Record, MDAIK 40 227- 235

Reeves 1990 — C. N. Reeves, Valley of the Kings : the Decline of a Royal Necropolis, Kegan Paul International: London

Schenkel 1978 — W. Schenkel, Die Bewässerungsrevolution im Alten Ägypten, Philipp von Zabern: Mainz am Rhein

Smith 2006 — M. Smith, the Great Decree issued to the Nome of the Silent Land, RdE 57, 217-232

Steinmann 1980 — F. Steinmann, Untersuchungen zu den handwerklich-künstlerischen Produktion beschäftigten Personen und Berufsgruppen des Neuen Reichs, ZÄS 107 (1980), 137-157

Sweeney 2001 — D. Sweeney, Correspondence and Dialogue: Pragmatic Factors in late Ramesside Letter-Writing, ÄAT 49, Harrassowitz: Wiesbaden

Tosi & Roccati 1972 — M. Tosi & A. Roccati, Stele e altre epigrafi di Deir el Medina : n. 50001 - n. 50262. Edizioni d'arte fratelli Pozzo: Torino

Urk VII — Sethe 1935 K. H. Sethe, Historisch-biographische Urkunden des Mittleren Reiches, HeftI, Urkunden des ägyptischen Altertums VII, J. C. Hinrichs: Leipzig

Valbelle 1975 — D. Valbelle, La tombe de Ḥay à Deir El-Médina (N° 267), MIFAO 95, IFAO : Le Caire

Valbelle 1976 — D. Valbelle, Remarques sur les textes néo-égyptiens non littéraires, BIFAO 76, 101-109

Valbelle 1977a — D. Valbelle, Catalogue des poids à inscriptions hiérartiques de Deir el-Médineh : nos 5001-5423, DFIFAO 16 IFAO:1977

Valbelle 1977b — D. Valbelle, Remarques sur les textes néo-égyptiens non littéraires, BIFAO 77, 129-136

Vandier 1950 — J. Vandier, Mo'alla : la tombe d'Ankhtifi et la tombe de Sébekhotep, BdE 18 IFAO : Le Caire

Vandier 1977 — J. Vandier, Ramsés-Siptah, RdE 23, 165-191

Ventura 1986 — R. Ventura, Living in a City of the Dead : a Selection of Topographical and Administrative Terms in the Documents of the Theban Necropolis, OBO 69, Universitätsverlag: Freiburg-Vandenhoeck & Ruprecht: Göttingen-Freiburg

Verhoeven 2001 — U. Verhoeven, Untersuchungen zur späthieratischen Buchschrift, OLA 99, Uitgeverij Peeters: Leuven

Vernus 1994 — P. Vernus, Observations sur le titre *imy-rꜥ ḫtmt* « directeur du Tresor », S. Allam (ed.), Grund und Boden in Altägypten (rechtliche und sozio-ökonomishce Verhältnisse). Akten des internationalen Symposium Tübingen 18.-20. Juni 1990, Tübingen 1994, 251-260

Viitala 2001 — J. Toivari-Viitala, Women at Deir el-Medina. A study of the Status and Roles of the Female Inhabitants in the Workmen's community during the Ramesside Period, EU 15, NINO: Leiden

Vogelsang & Gardiner 1908 — F. Vogelsang & A.H. Gardiner, Literarische Texte des Mittleren Reiches. I. Die Klagen des Bauern, J. C. Hinrichs'sche Buchhandlung: Leipzig

Wb — Ermann & Grapow 1935-1971 A. Erman & H. Grapow, Wörterbuch der aegyptischen Sprache, vols I-V, Akademie Verlag Berlin: Berlin

Ward 1982 — W.A. Ward, Index of Egyptian Administrative and Religious Titles of the Middle Kingdom: with a Glossary of Words and Phrases used, American University of Beirut: Beirut

Ward 1994 — W. A. Ward, Foreigners living in the Village, in L. H. Lesko ed., Pharaoh's Workers the villagers of Deir el Medina, Cornell University Press: Ithaca and London, 61-85

Weeks 2000 — K. R. Weeks ed., KV 5: A Preliminary Report on the Excavation of the Tomb of the Sons of Ramses II in the Valley of the Kings, vols I-II, Publication of the Theban Mapping Project 2, American University in Cairo Press: Cairo and

Wente 1967 — E. F. Wente, Late Ramesside Letters, Chicago UP: Chicago (Ill.)

Wente 1990 — E. F. Wente, Letters from Ancient Egypt, Writings from the ancient Worlds/Society of Biblica Literature, Scholars Press: Atlanta

Wimmer 1995 — S. Wimmer, Hieratische Paläographie der nicht-literarischen Ostraka der 19. und 20. Dynastie, ÄAT 28, Harrassowitz in Kommission: Wiesbaden

Winfried 1968 — B. Winfried, Aufbau bedeutung der altägyptischen opferformel, J. J. Augustin: New York

Winlock 1912 — H. E. Winlock, The work of the Egyptian Expedition, BMMA 7, 184-90

INDEXES

Names of gods		
*R*a	deity	21, 37, 59, 60, 61
Names of kings		
Amenmesse		4, 5, 6, 17, 27, 28, 31, 32, 33, 34, 35, 62, 66, 69
Bay	Chancelor of the entire land (king?)	61, 67, 68
Merenptah		5, 6, 18, 21, 32, 56, 57, 65, 67
Ramses II		6, 15, 19, 27, 31, 34, 38, 44, 45, 50, 55, 56, 57, 58, 62, 68
Ramses III		5, 15, 17, 18, 19, 23, 27, 31, 32, 44, 45, 60, 66, 67, 68
Ramses IV		52, 64
Ramses V		6
Ramses VI		6, 31, 48, 50, 51, 58, 64, 66, 67, 68
Ramses VII		20
Ramses IX		19
Ramses X		67
Ramses XI		19, 62
Seti II		17, 21, 23, 26, 31, 32, 48, 62, 67, 68
Setnakhte		23, 61
Siptah		4, 6, 19, 20, 23, 27, 28, 31, 32, 33, 35, 36, 42, 56, 61, 62, 66, 67, 68, 69
Tausert		27, 36, 61
Royal epithets		
ꜥꜣ nry	great of Terror	48
Ramses II's sons		
Wr-mꜣ	prince	55, 57
Mry-mn-tiw	prince	55, 56
Nb-n	prince	55, 58
Rꜥ-mry	prince	55, 57
Rꜥ-msw-pꜣ it-nṯr	prince	55, 58
sꜣ-ptḥ	prince	55, 56
snḫt-n-imn	prince	55, 56
Index of titles		
imi-r iḥ(.w)	Overseer of the cattle	50, 53
imi-r mr	Overseer	50, 53

	of (?)	
imi-r- nw.w	Overseer of the hunters	50, 53
imi-r st	Overseer of the storehouse	50, 53
imi-r k3.t	Overseer of the building activity	50, 53
ḥry- iḥw	Superior of the cattle	49, 51
ḥry-is.t	Superior of the gang	49, 51
ḥry-ꜥẖ	Superior of the burnt offerings	49, 52
ḥry-(nf) ww	Superior of the sailors	49, 52
ḥry-b3ky.w	Superior of the royal works	49, 52
ḥry-bit	Superior of the bees	49, 52
ḥry-pr-šnꜥ	Superior of the storehouse	49, 51
ḥry-mr(.t)	Superior of the servants	49, 51
ḥry-mz b	Superior of the (?) carriers	49, 51
ḥry-mz wdn.w	Superior of the stable	49, 52, 53
ḥry-md̠3y	Superior of the police	6, 49, 51
ḥry-nw.w	Superior of the hunters	49, 52
ḥry-ẖ3(w.t)	Superior of the offering tables	49, 53
ḥry-ẖꜥḳ	Superior of the barbers	49, 52, 53

Personal names listed in the corpus

Ỉpwy	Draftsman	29, 32, 33
Ỉmn-m-ipt	no title	15, 24, 26
Ỉmn-ẖꜥw s3 Ḥ3y	no title	16, 18
Ỉmn-(?)	no title	25
ꜥ3-nẖt.w	no title	24, 26

ꜥ3-pḥty	no title	24, 26
Wn-nfr (s3) Pn-imn	no title	16, 17, 18
P3-imi-r-iḥ.w	no title	3, 5, 6, 16, 19, 20, 24, 27
P3-ym.w	no title	24, 26
P3-nḫt-ꜥ3	no title	16, 19
P3-rꜥ-http = Rꜥ-ḥtp	no title	16, 18, 34, 35
P3-šdw	no title	18, 24, 26, 31
[P3] šdw s3 Ḥḥ(-nḫw)	no title	29, 31, 32
Pn-imn	no title	16, 17, 18
P[tḥ]-šdw	no title	24, 25
Pn-dw3ww	no title	29, 32
Mꜥ-k (y)-rmṯ-tw.f	no title	24, 25
Mn-n3	no title	16, 18
Mry-rꜥ or Rꜥ-mry	no title	6, 14, 15, 29, 31
N3-ḫy s3 Bw-ḳn-tw.f	no title	29, 32
Nb-imn	no title	29, 31
Nb-imn.t (t)	no title	16, 18, 19
Nb-nfr s3 W3d-ms	no title	24, 27
Nb-nḫt.w	no title	24, 26, 29
Nb-smn	no title	29, 31
Nḫw-m-mwt	no title	29, 31
Nḫt-imn	no title	16, 18
Nḫt-sw	no title	3, 4, 6
Rꜥw-wbn	no title	24, 27
Rw-tḫ	no title	25, 27
Ḥ3y	Chief of the gang	3, 5, 16, 18, 29, 32, 62
Ḥ3y	Draftsman	18
Ḥwy	no title	14, 15, 27
Ḥwy-nfr	no title	3, 5, 19, 24, 25, 27, 31, 35
Ḥwy s3 Ḥwy-nfr	no title	3, 5, 24, 25, 27, 31, 35
Ḥwy s3 Ḫꜥw	no title	24, 25, 27, 29, 32
Ḥrw	Vizier	21, 23
Ḥrw	no title	59, 60
Ḥrw-m-wi3	no title	3, 5, 24, 26, 29, 31
Ḥsi-sw-nb.f	no title	5, 6, 15, 24, 25, 27
Ḥtpw	no title	24, 25
Ḫ3mw = Ḫ3my	no title	25, 31
Ḫꜥ[...]	no title	3, 4
Ḫꜥ-m-ip.t	no title	16, 18
Ḫꜥ–m-nwn	Superior	3, 5, 6
Ḫꜥ-m-nwn	no tite	27
Ḫnm-m-sw	no title	3, 5
Ḫnmw-msw	no title	19, 24, 26
Ḫnmw-nḫt	no title	16, 18
s3-w3ḏyt	no title	29, 31, 32, 33
sbk-ms	no title	16, 18
[K3] s3 Rꜥ-(ms)	no title	24, 26
K3r	Scribe	37
K3-s3	no title	24, 26
Ḳ3-ḥ3	no title	25, 26, 28
Ḳn	no title	29, 31
(?)s3 Pn-nbw	no title	24

Documents quoted

Ostraca

O. Ashm 36	12
O. Ashm 160	12 (footnote 70)
O. Ashm 254	12
O. Ashm 266	12 (footnote 70)
O. Ashm 267	12 (footnote 70)
O. Ashm 268	12 (footnote 70)
O. Ashm 269	12 (footnote 70)
O. Ashm 270	12 (footnote 70)
O. Ashm 285	13 (footnote 74)
O. Berlin P 10634	38
O. Berlin P 12294	38
O. Berlin P 14885	52
O. BM EA 5634	19
O. BM EA 50730	6, 51
O. BM EA 50745	6, 51
O. BM EA 65599	41
O. BM EA 65600	41
O. Cairo Carnarvon 421	9
O. Cairo Carnarvon 343	26
O. Cairo CG 25008	67
O. Cairo CG 25013	67
O. Cairo GC 25020-25023	67
O. Cairo CG 25055	67
O. Cairo CG 25069	67
O. Cairo CG 25973	67
O. Cairo CG 25081	67
O. Cairo CG 25089	67
O. Cairo CG 25104	67
O. Cairo CG 25112	67
O. Cairo CG 25127	67
O. Cairo CG 25178-25180	67
O. Cairo CG 25189bis	67
O. Cairo CG 25228	67
O. Cairo CG 25237	4
O. Cairo CG 25247	12 (footnote 70)
O. Cairo CG 25249	67
O. Cairo CG 25248-25249	67
O. Cairo CG 25257	12 (footnote 70)
O. Cairo CG 25269	67
O. Cairo CG 25293	67
O. Cairo CG 25297-25398	67
O. Cairo CG 25313-25315	67
O. Cairo CG 25321	67
O. Cairo CG 25331	40, 41
O. Cairo CG 25352	68
O. Cairo CG 25354	67

O. Cairo CG 25357 67
O. Cairo CG 25258 13 (footnote 74)
O. Cairo CG 25360 67
O. Cairo CG 25362 67
O. Cairo CG 25364 67
O. Cairo CG 25512 32 (footnote 203)
O. Cairo CG 25513 27
O. Cairo CG 25517 26
O. Cairo CG 25519 26, 35, 33 (footnote 209), 35 (footnote 217)
O. Cairo CG 25520 33 (209)
O. Cairo CG 25521 4, 27, 35, 68, 35 (footnote 217)
O. Cairo CG 25522 33 (209), 35
O. Cairo CG 25523 26
O. Cairo CG 25553 19, 61
O. Cairo CG 25556 17
O. Cairo CG 25558 41
O. Cairo CG 25560 61
O. Cairo CG 25561 23 (footnote 138)
O. Cairo CG 25571 67
O. Cairo CG 25576 61
O. Cairo CG 25577 61
O. Cairo CG 25599 67
O. Cairo CG 25626 67
O. Cairo CG 25628 67
O. Cairo CG 25629 67
O. Cairo CG 25634 67
O. Cairo CG 25642 61
O. Cairo CG 25644 23 (footnote 138)
O. Cairo CG 25648 67
O. Cairo CG 25657 67
O. Cairo CG 25672 61
O. Cairo CG 25742 12
O. Cairo CG 25744 61
O. Cairo CG 25760 50, 51
O. Cairo CG 25764 51
O. Cairo CG 25766 61, 68
O. Cairo CG 25779 26, 32 (footnotes 199, 202)
O. Cairo CG 25780 27 (footnote 164)
O. Cairo CG 25782 35, 32 (footnote 199)
O. Cairo CG 25783 4
O. Cairo CG 25788 68
O. Cairo CG 25789 68
O. Cairo CG 25797 26
O. Cairo CG 25781 26
O. Cairo CG 25802 50 (footnote 264), 58
O. Cairo CG 25804 18
O. Cairo CG 25805 50 (footnote 264)
O. Cairo CG 25807 58
O. Cairo CG 25809 50 (footnote 264), 58
O. Cairo CG 25813 58
O. Cairo CG 25816 58
O. Cairo CG 25831 42
O. Cairo CG 25873 32
O. Cairo CG 51514 30

O. Cairo JE 72453 9
O. Cairo JE 72473 41
O. Cairo JE 72491 41
O. Černy 7 27, 32
O. DeM 60 19
O. DeM 114 22
O. DeM 144 7
O. DeM 159 7
O. DeM 209 30
O. DeM 236 17
O. DeM 246 60
O. DeM 269 6
O. DeM 286 19
O. DeM 290 4, 5, 6
O. DeM 556 18
O. DeM 580 18
O. DeM 621 19
O. DeM 831 18
O. DeM 900 32
O. DeM 912 26
O. DeM 929 9
O. DeM 10026 52
O. DeM 10046 18
O. DeM 10097 4
O. DeM 10102 9
O. DeM 1248 22
O. Gardiner 57 18
O. Gardiner 87 32
O. Gardiner 37 27 (footnote 167)
O. IFAO 371 19
O. IFAO 1080 19
O. Medelhavsmuseet MM 14126 27
O. Michaelides 2 19
O. Michaelides 5 18
O. Toronto B 7 5
O. Toronto A11 11
O. Turin N. 57082 31
O. Turin N. 57366 9
O. Turin N. 57381 12
O. Turin 57388 26 (footnote 144)
O. UC 39658 52

Papyri

P. Berlin P 10496 17, 19
P. Berlin P 14448 32
P. BM EA 75015 51
P. DeM 32 31
P. Leiden I, 348 22
P. New York MMA 35.9.21 38
P. Salt 124 31, 26 (footnote 158)
P. Turin Cat. 1880 18
P. Turin. Cat. 1898 19
P. Turin Cat. 1926 19
P. Turin Cat.1937 19

P. Turin Cat. 2071/224 + 1960 38
P. Turin Cat. 2094 19
P. Turin Cat. 54021 19

Figure 1a

KVO 1 recto

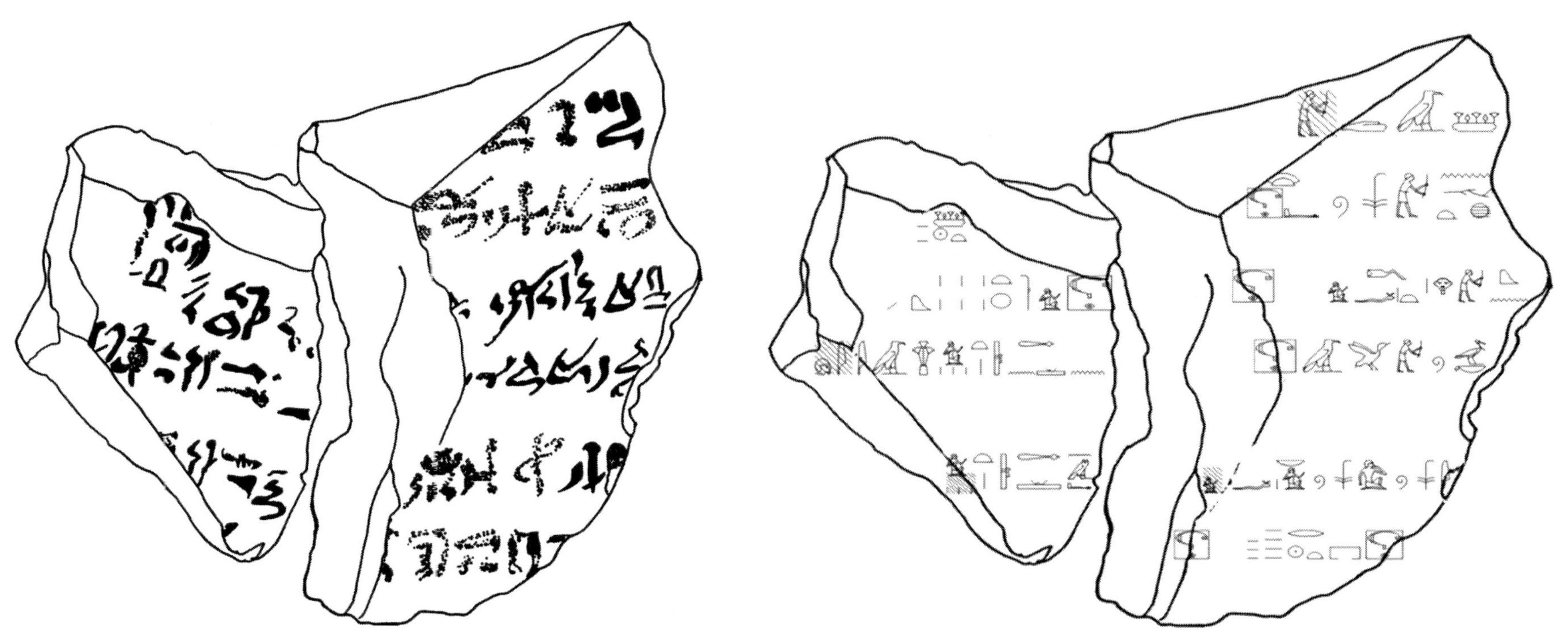

Figure 1b

KVO 1 verso

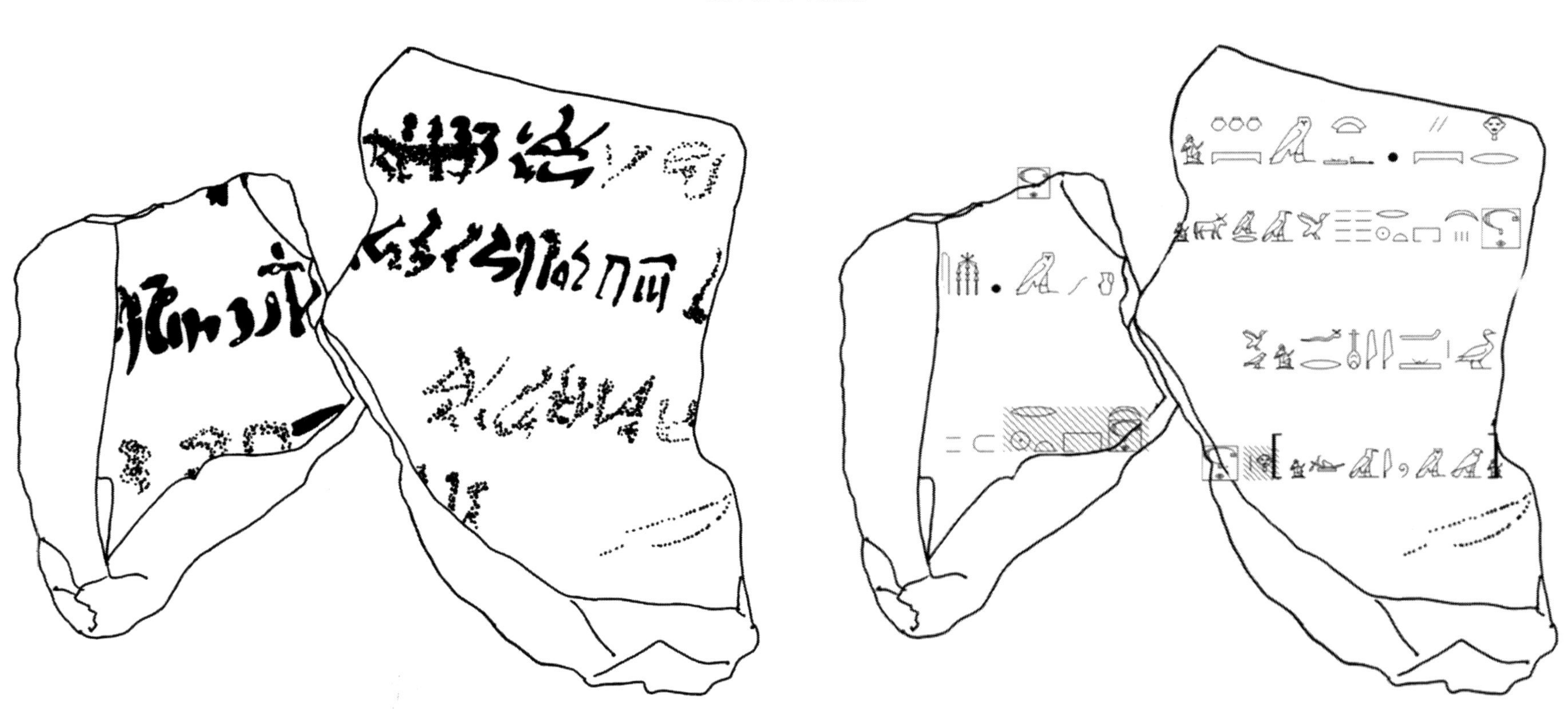

Figure 2a

KVO 2 recto

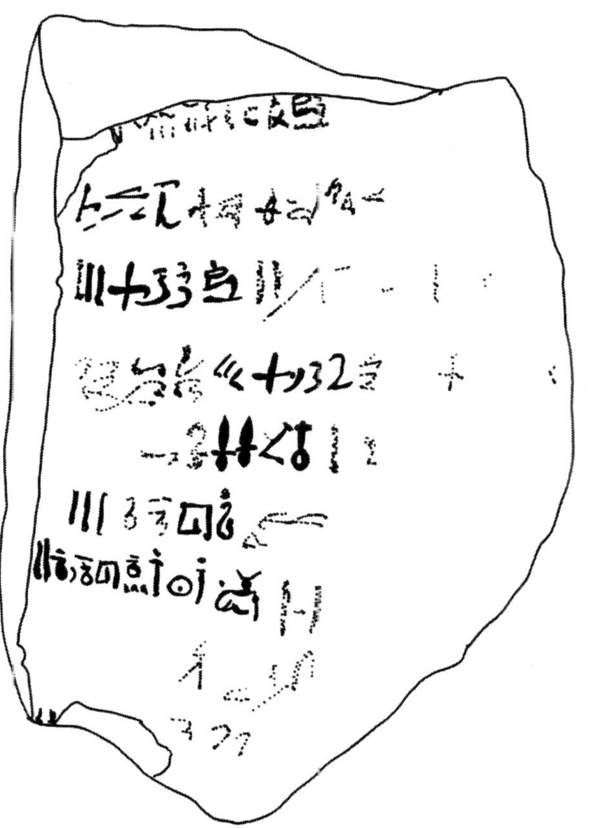

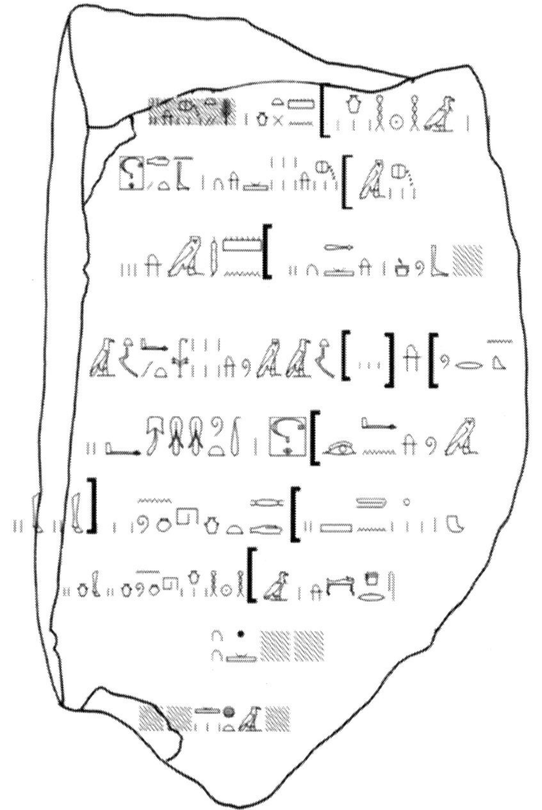

Figure 2b

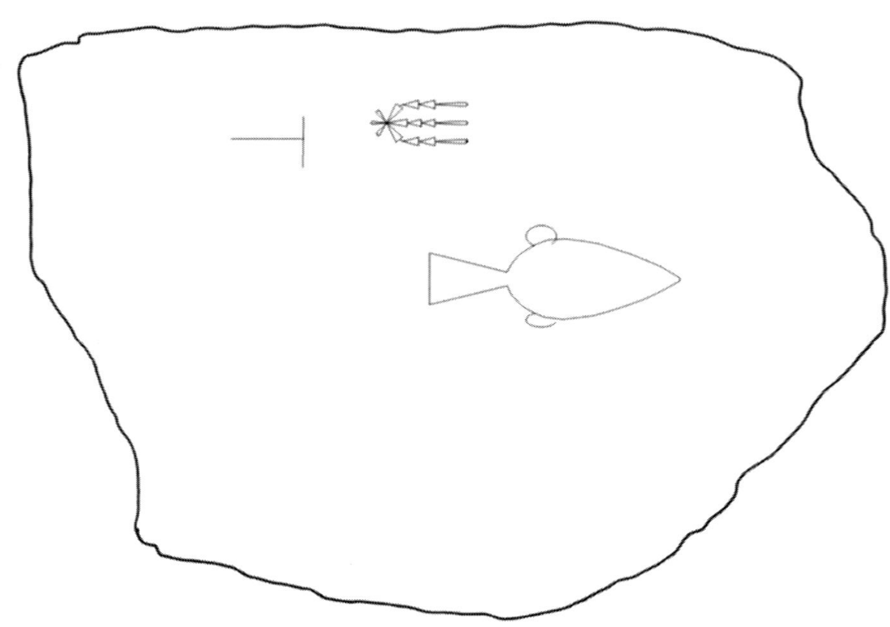

KVO 2 verso

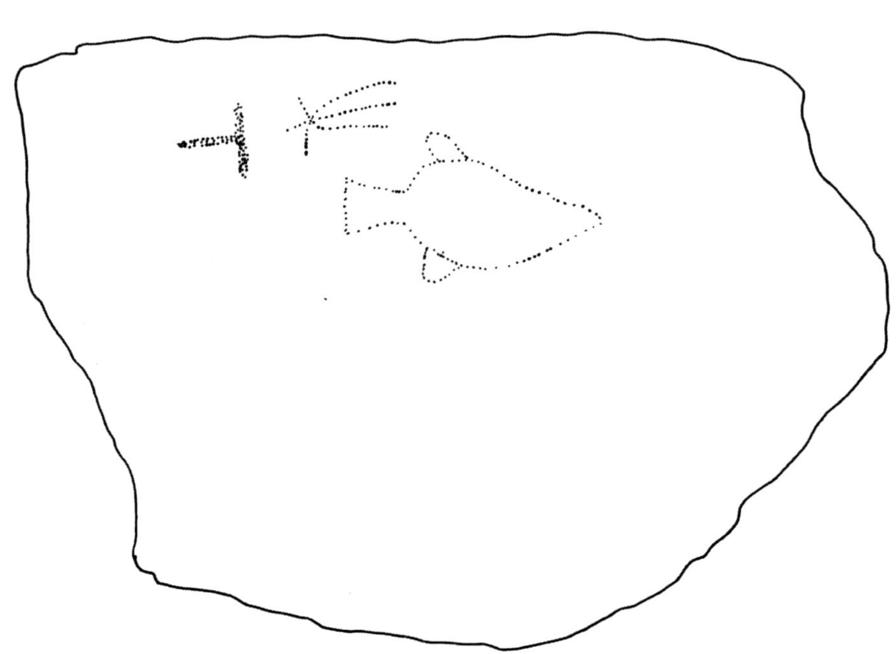

Figure 3

KVO 3

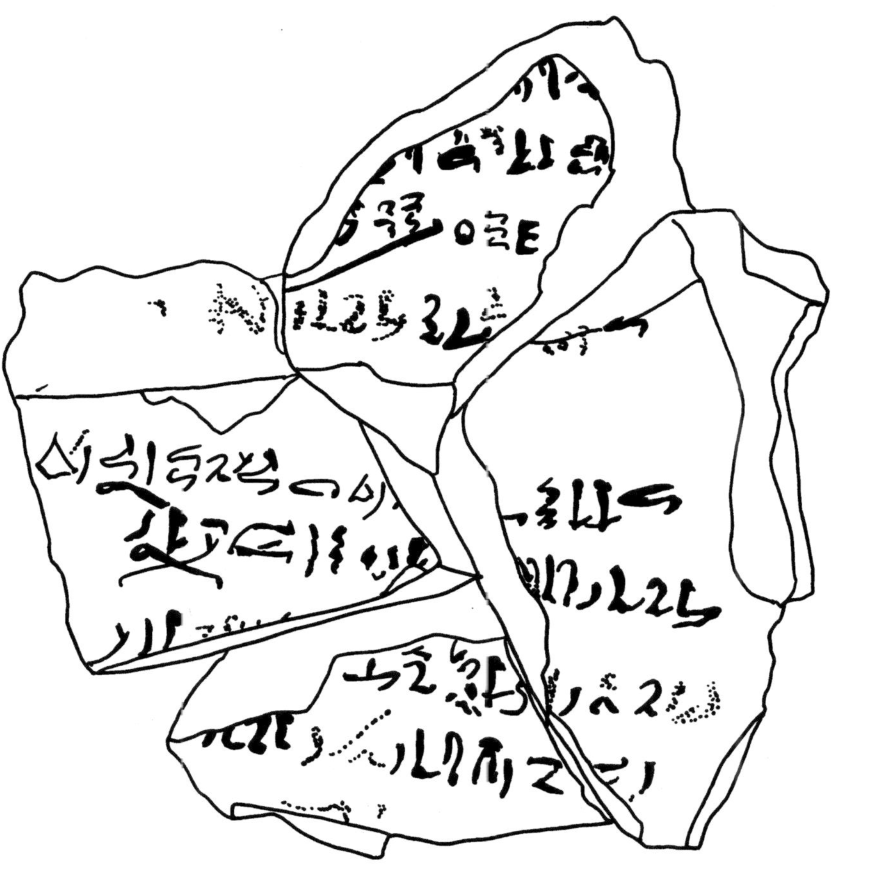

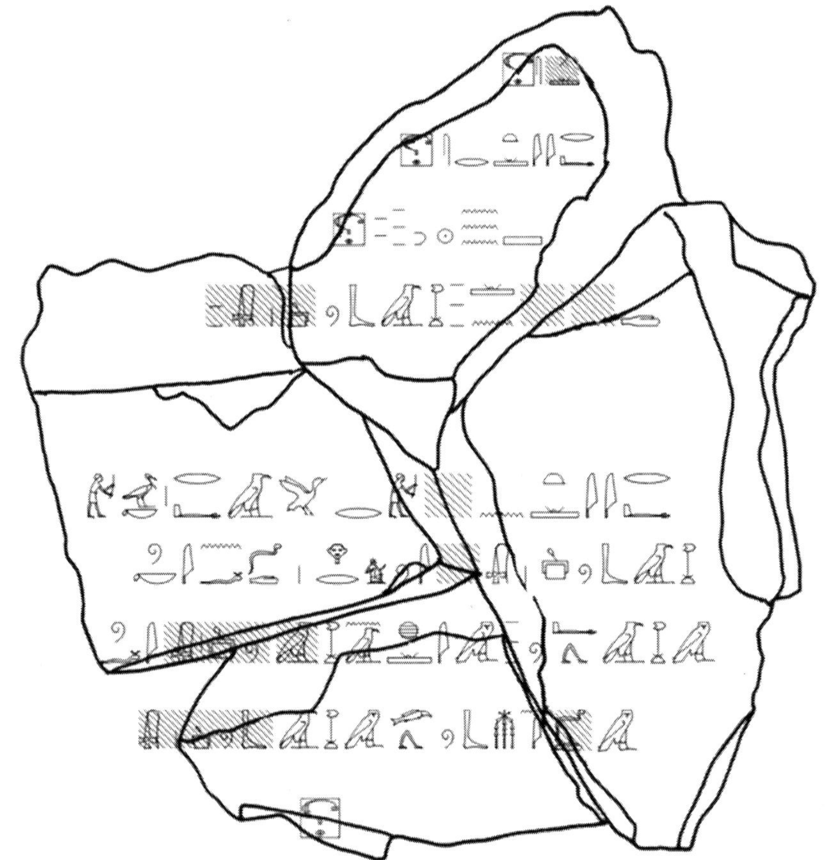

Figure 4a

KVO 4 recto

Figure 4b

KVO 4 verso

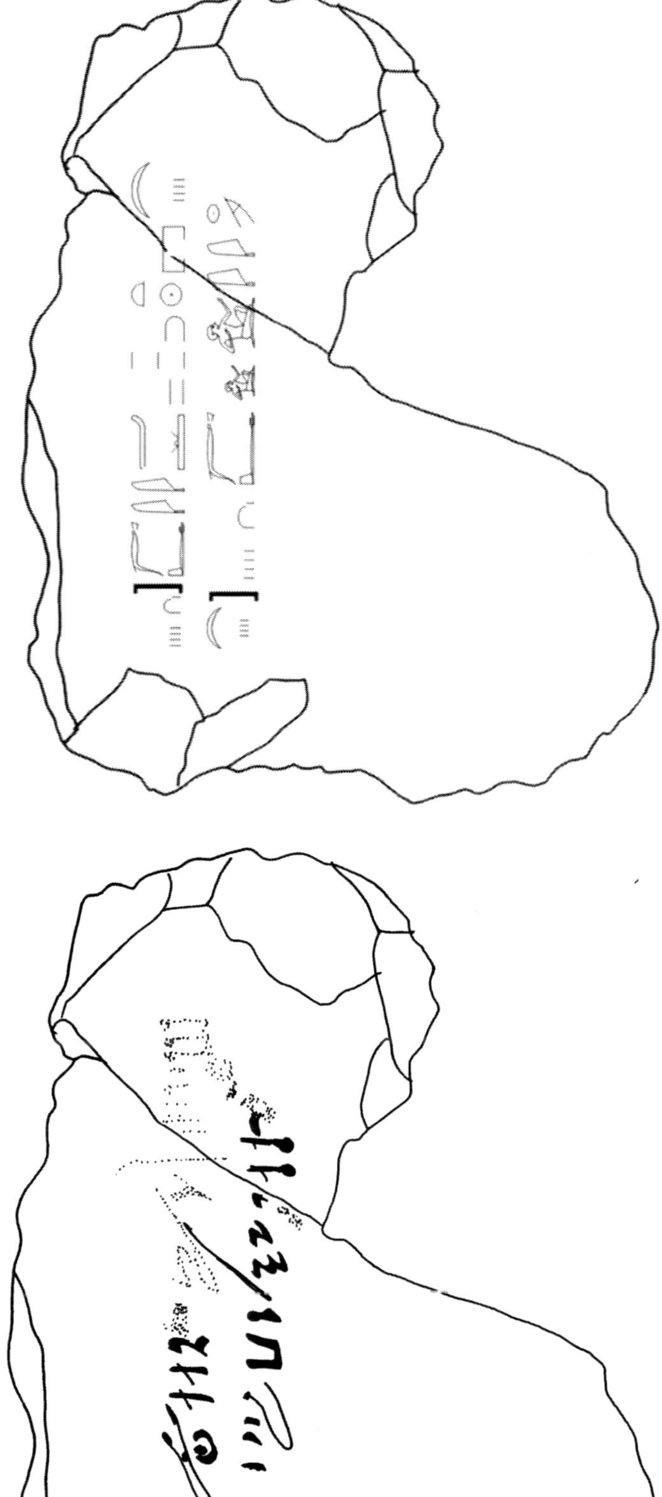

Figure 5a

KVO 5 recto

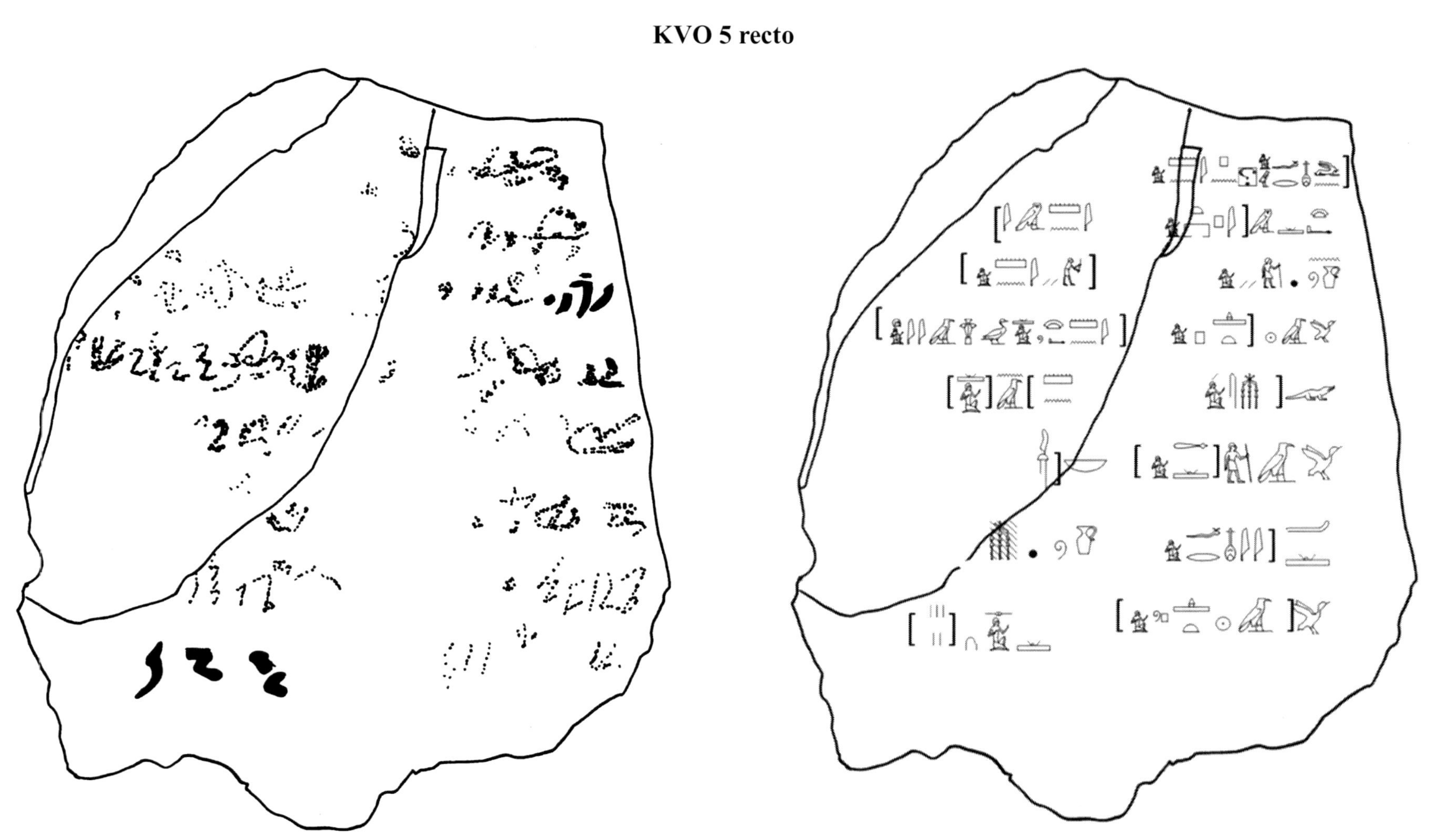

Figure 5b

KVO 5 verso

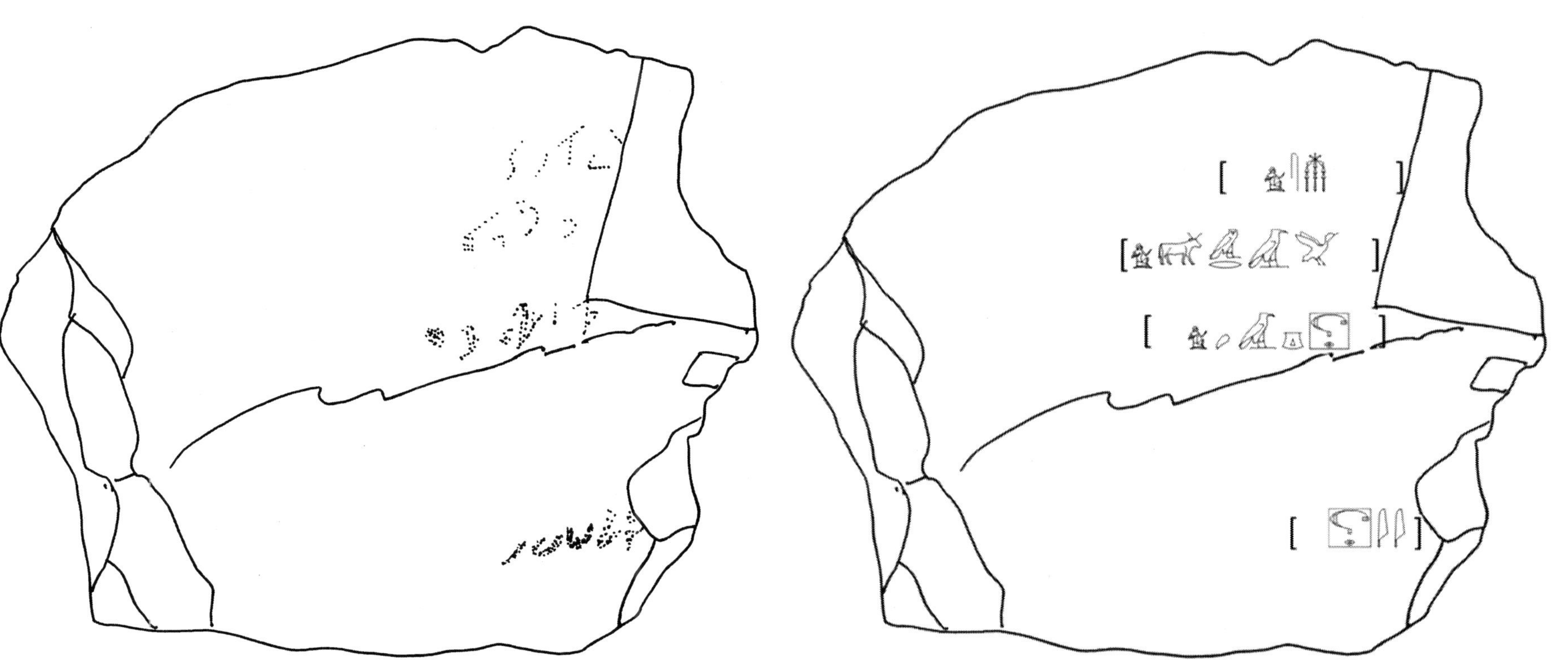

Figure 6

KVO 6

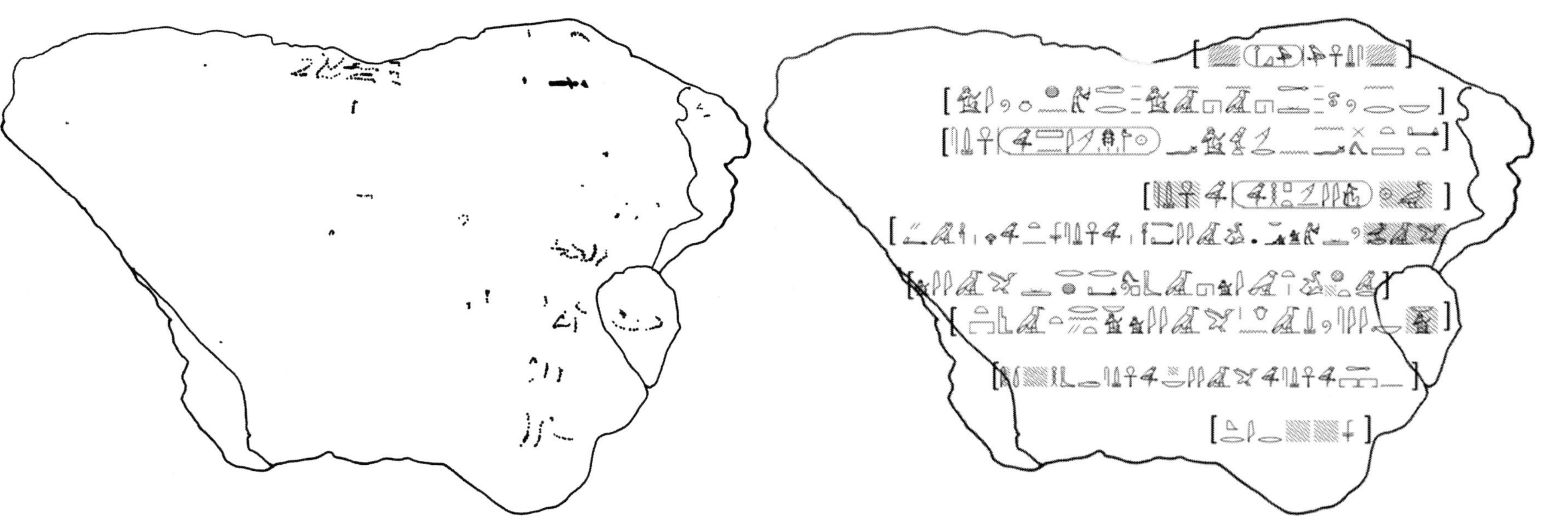

Figure 7a

KVO 7 recto

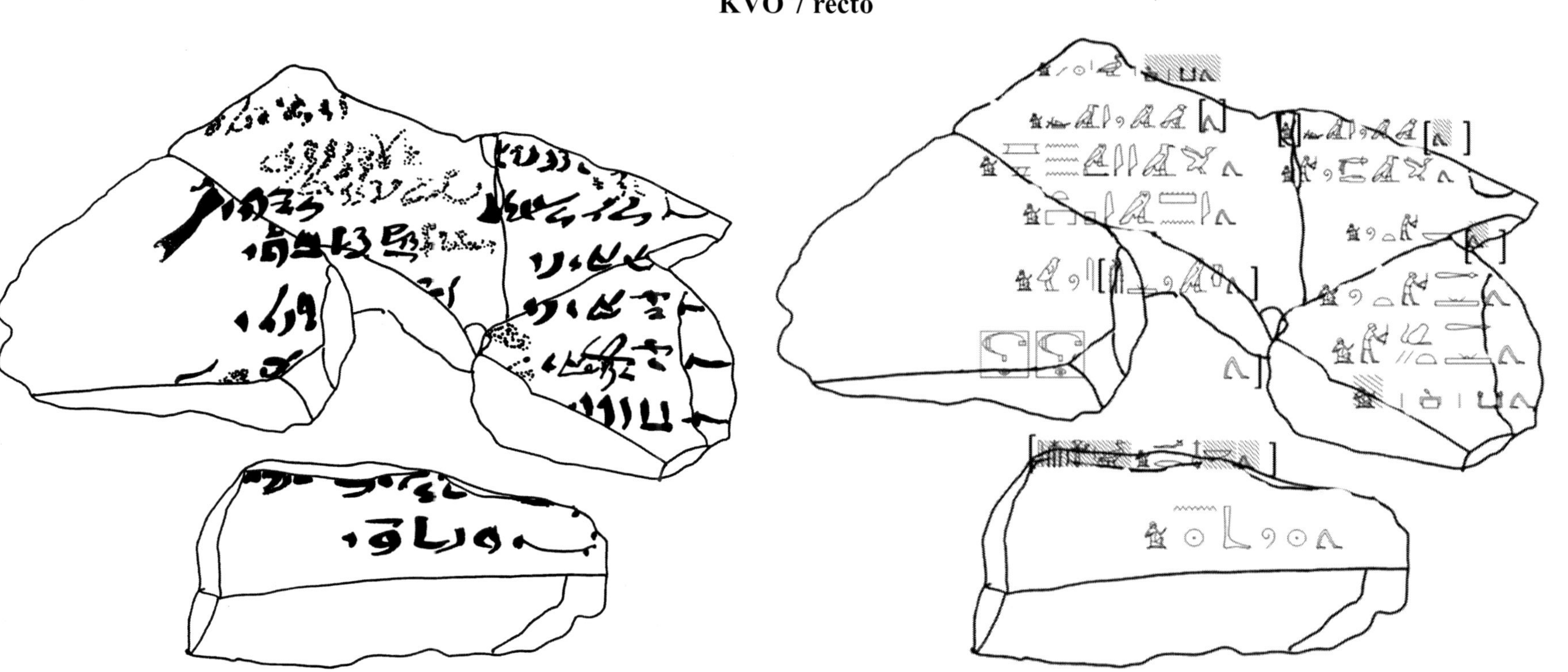

Figure 7b

KVO 7 verso

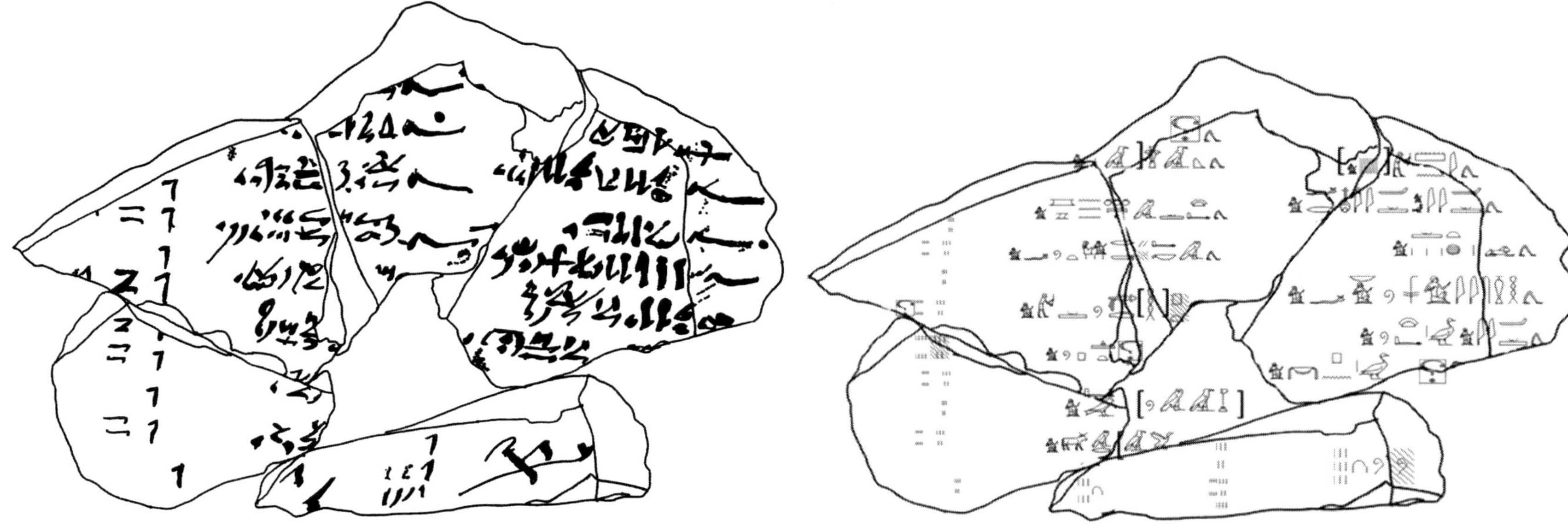

Figure 8a

KVO 8 recto

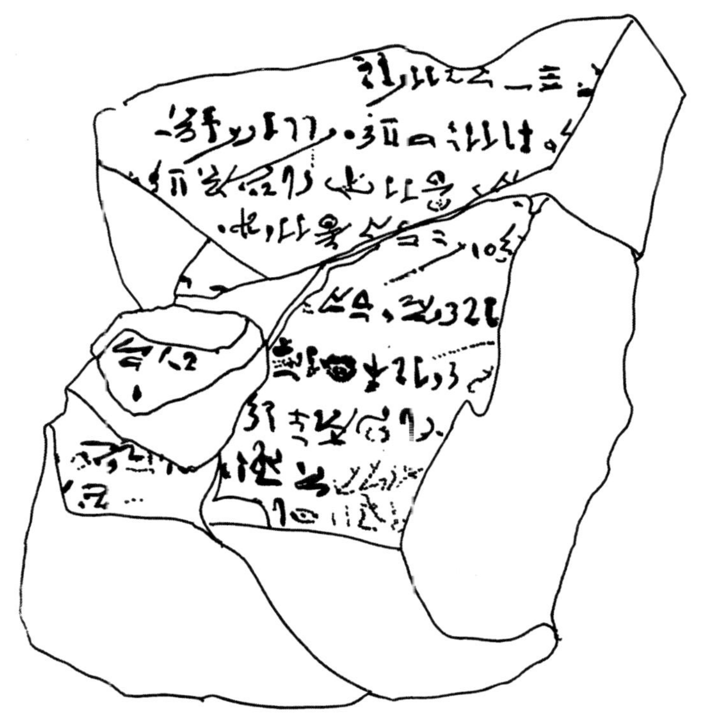

Figure 8b

KVO 8 verso

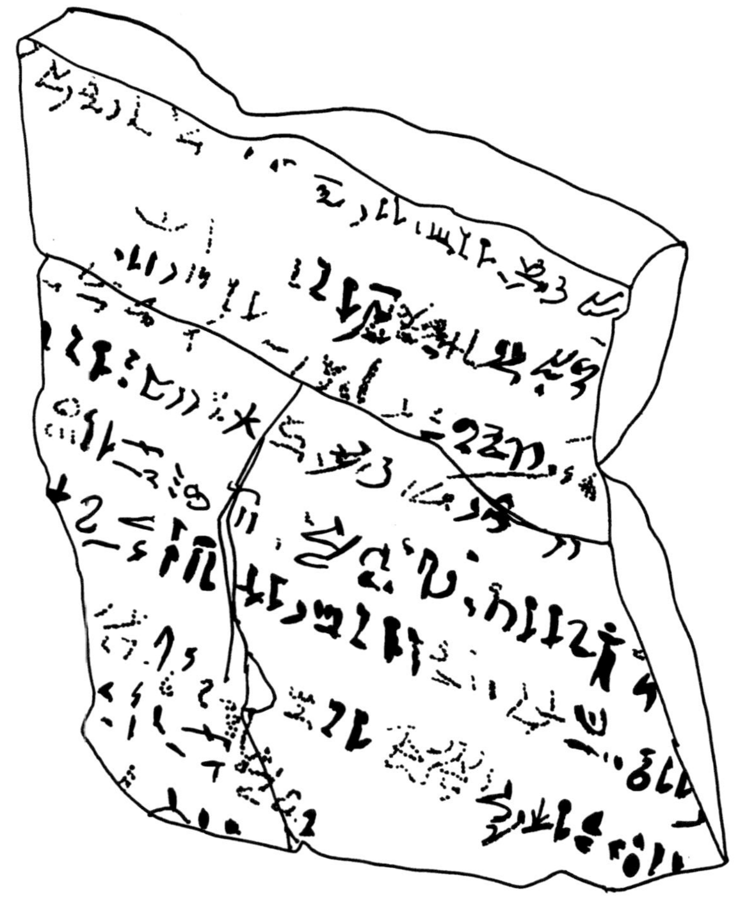

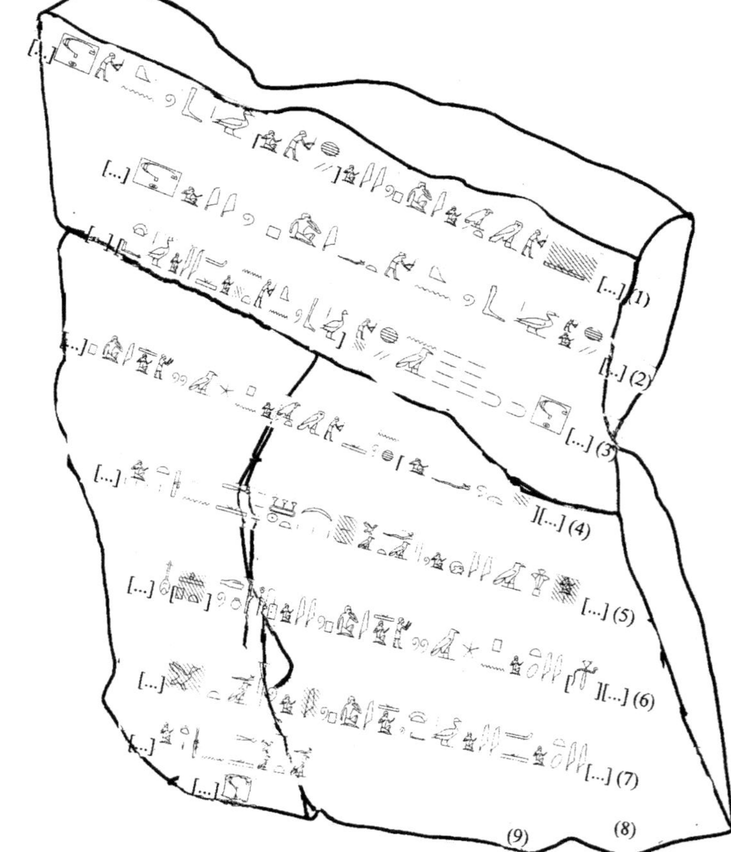

Figure 9

KVO 9

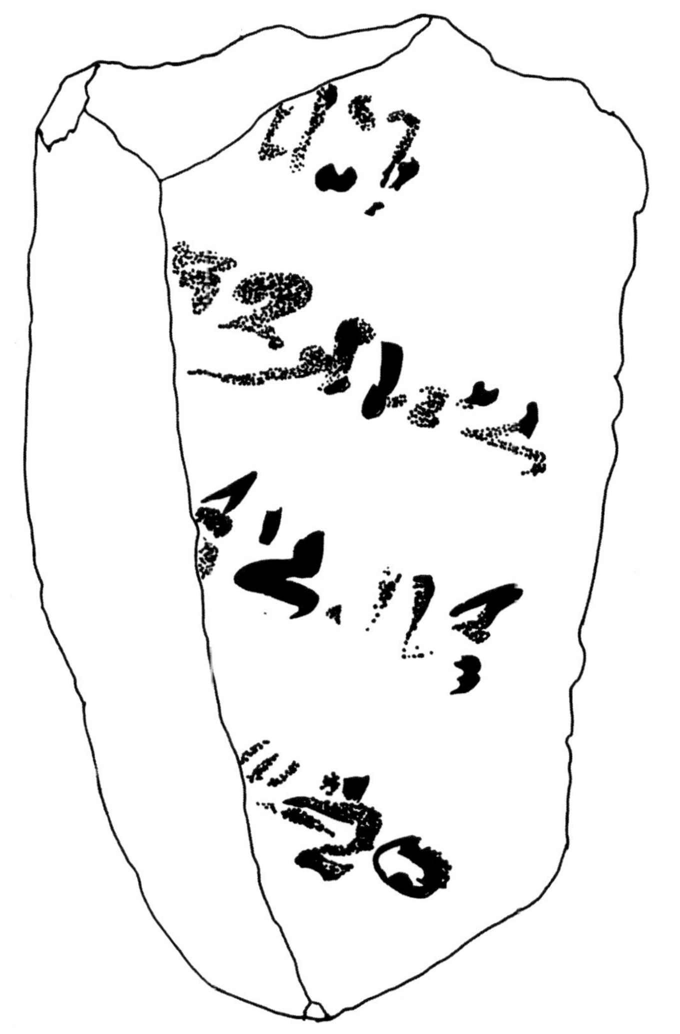

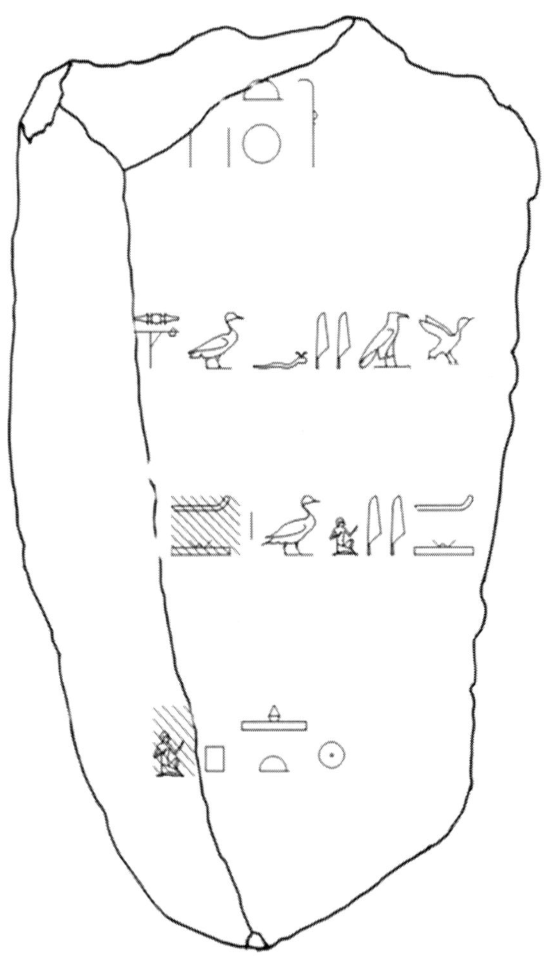

Figure 10

KVO 10

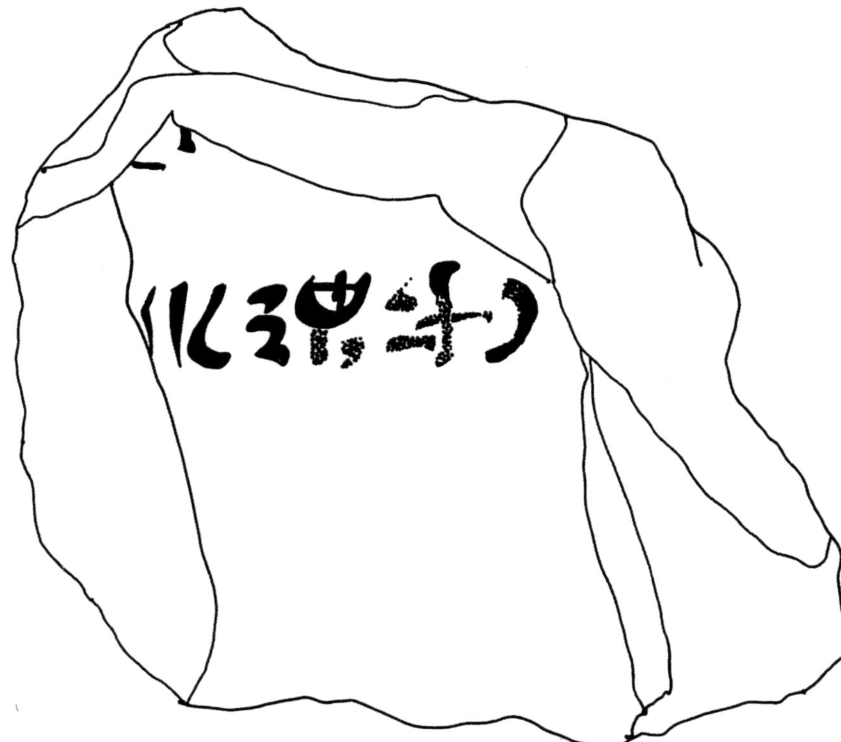

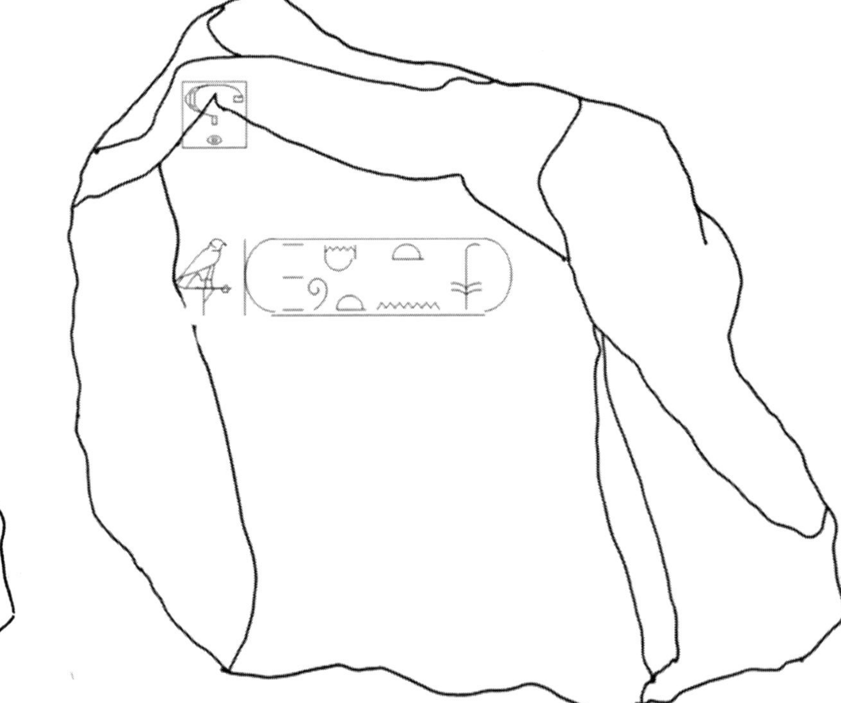

Figure 11

KVO 11

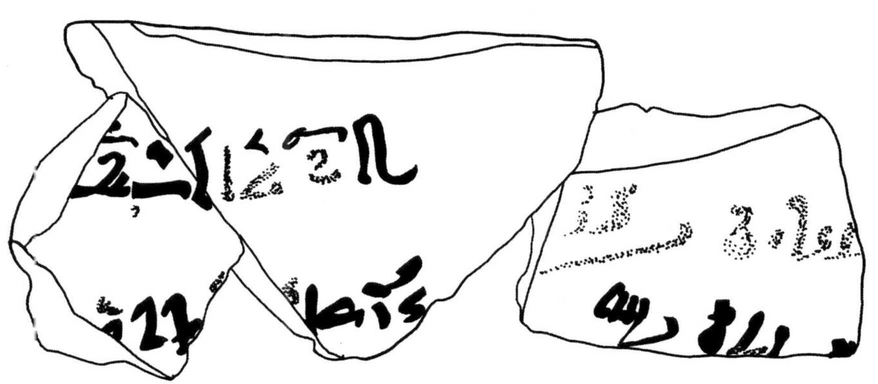

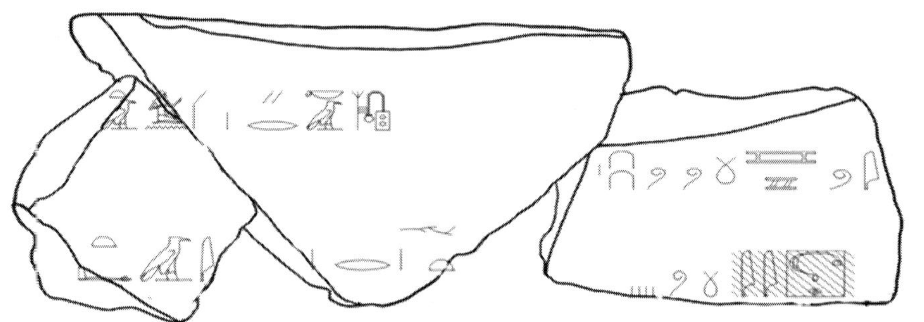

Figure 12a

KVO 12 recto

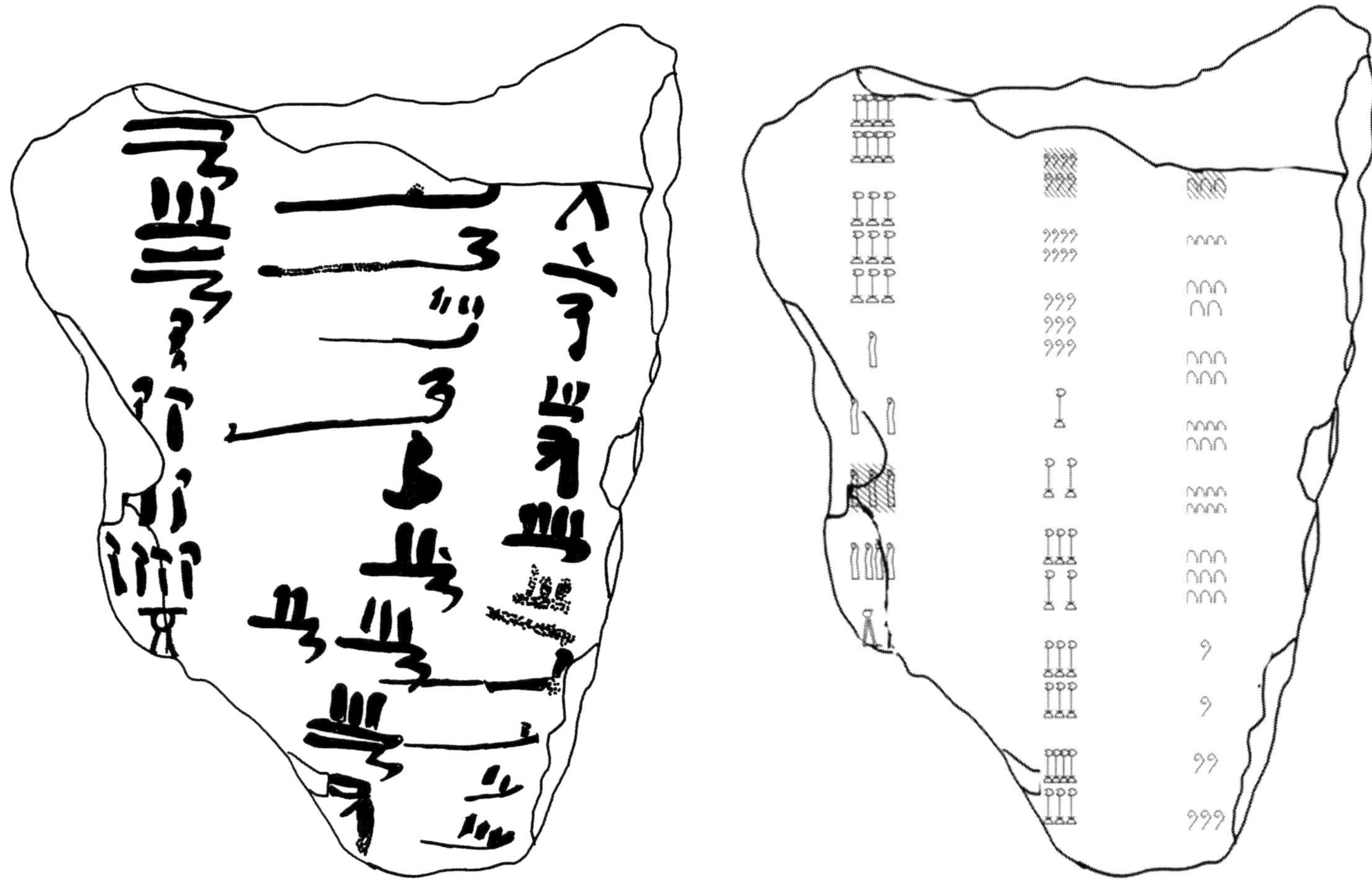

Figure 12b

KVO 12 verso

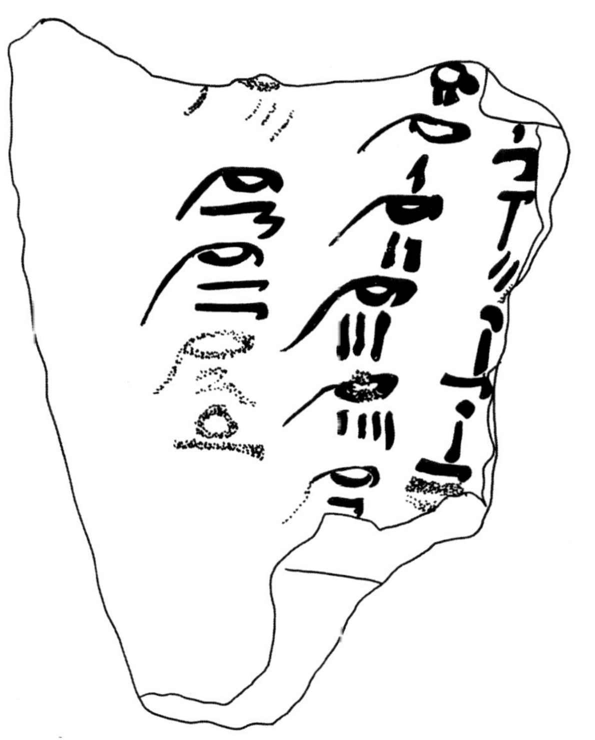

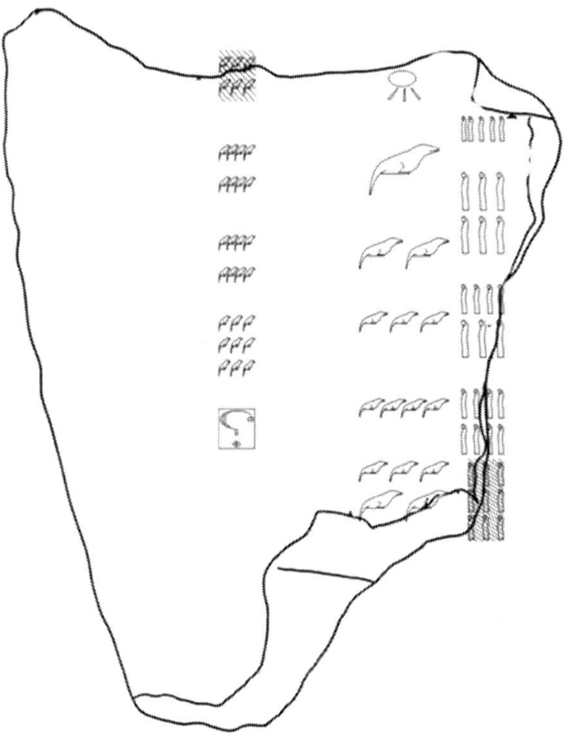

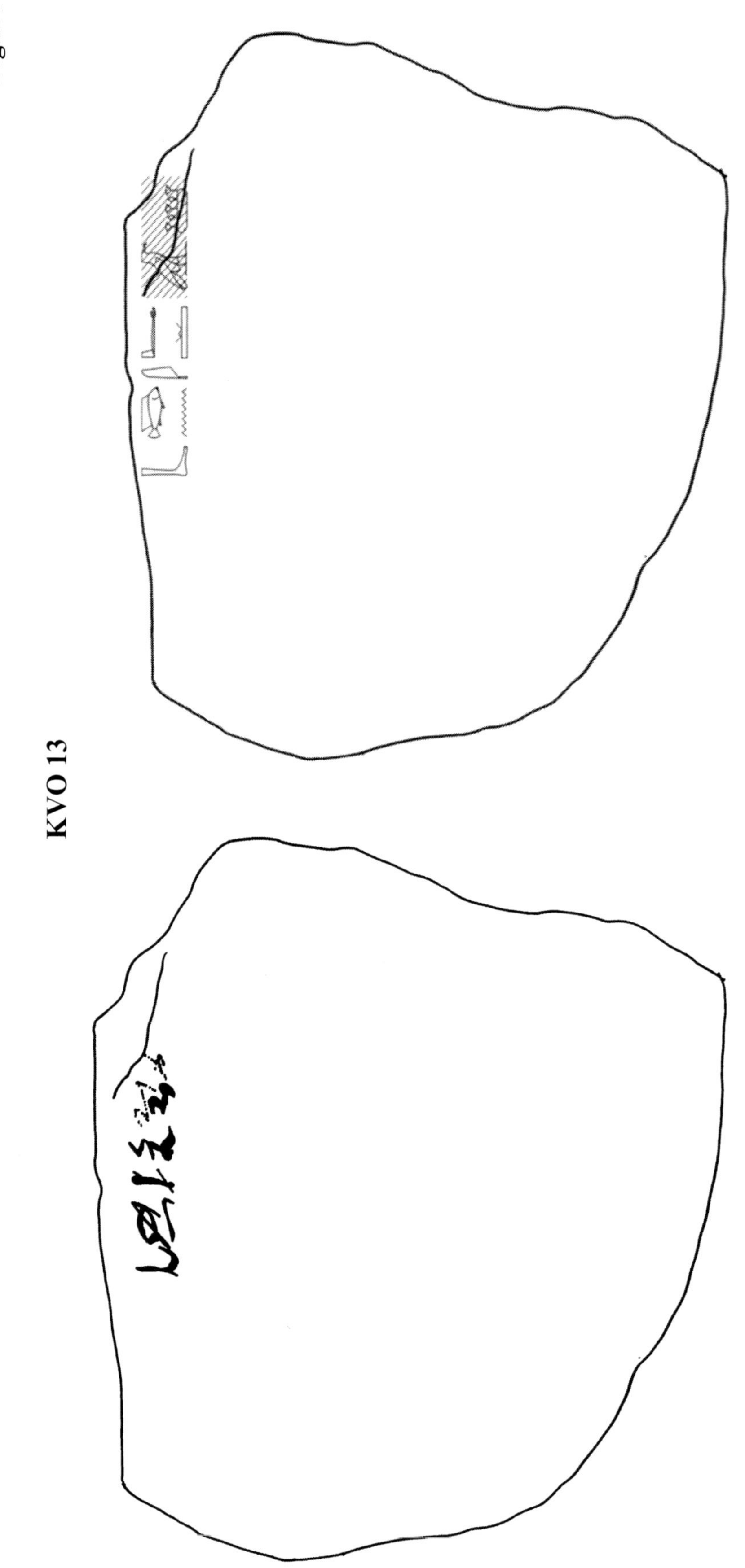

Figure 13

KVO 13

Figure 14

KVO 14

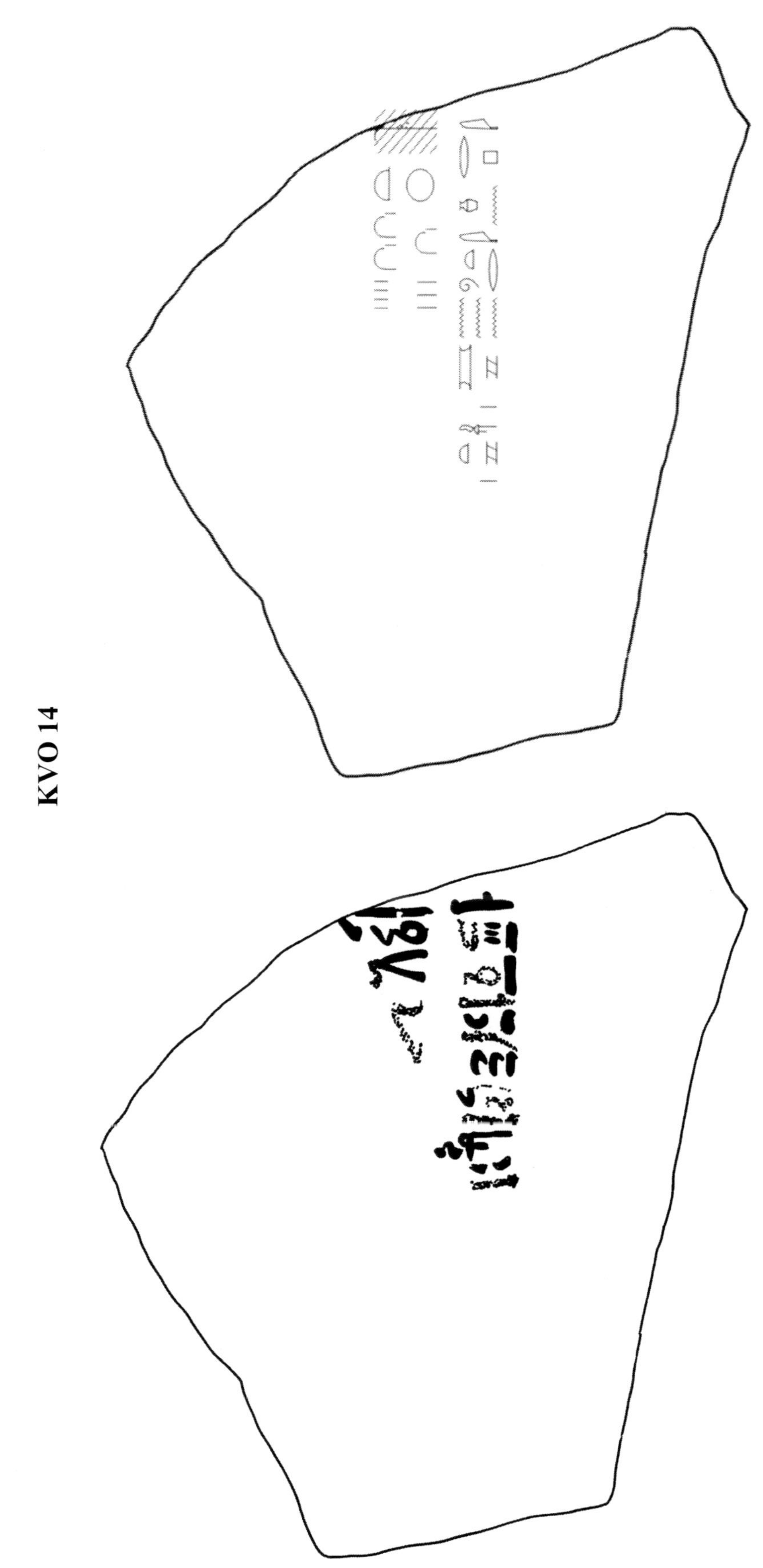

Figure 15

KVO 15

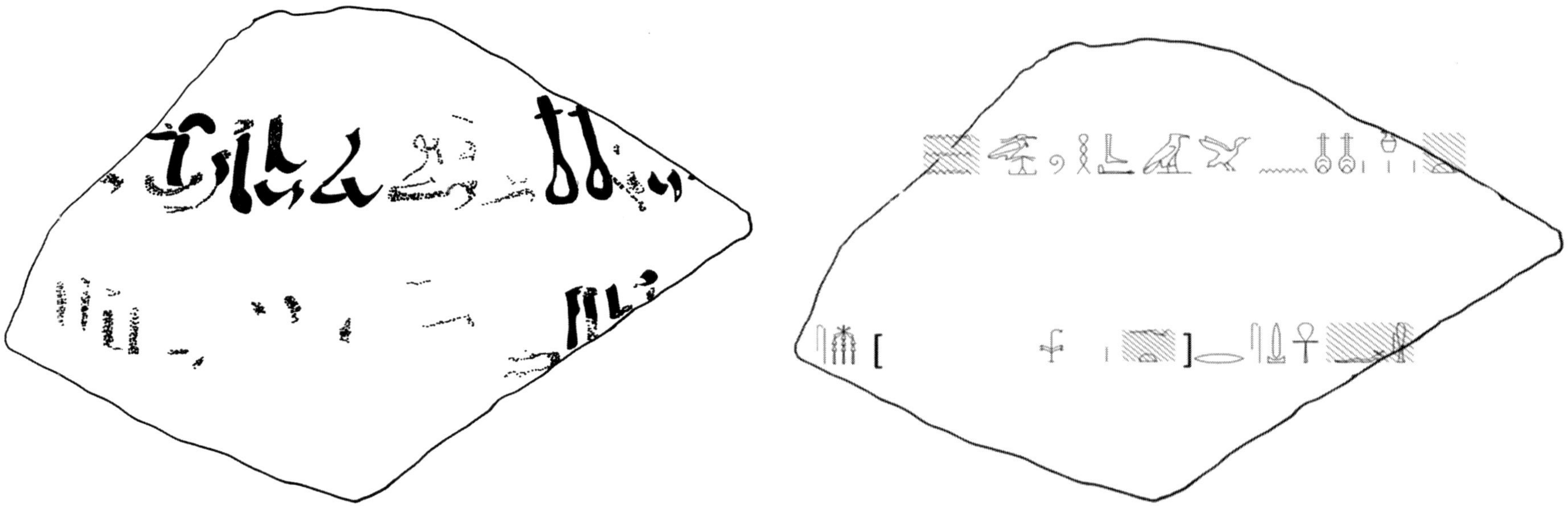

KVO 16

Figure 17a

KVO 17 recto

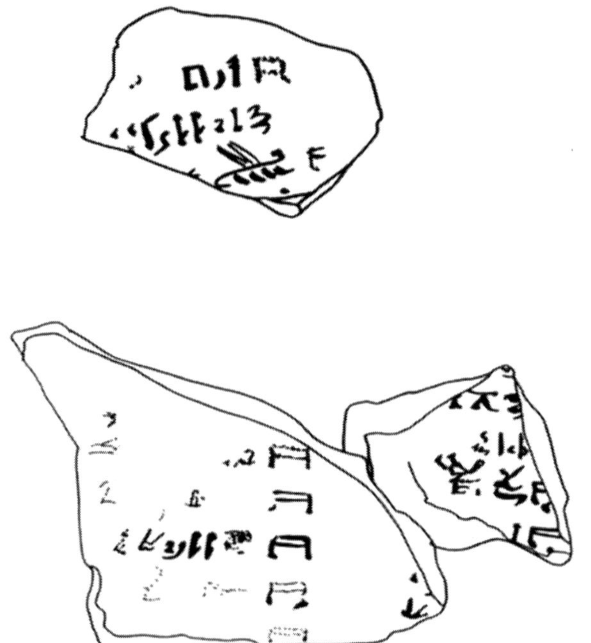

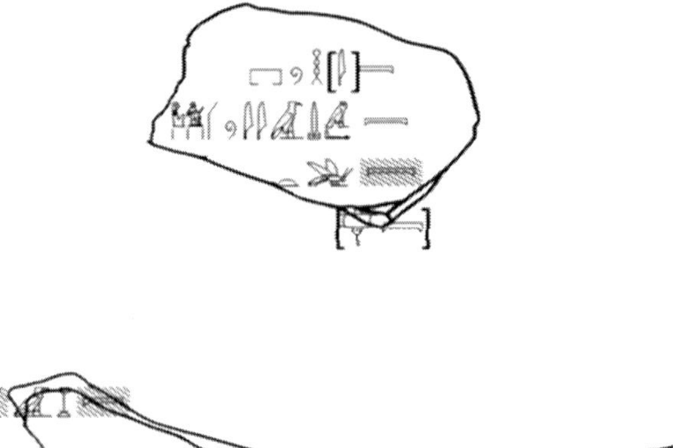

Figure 17b

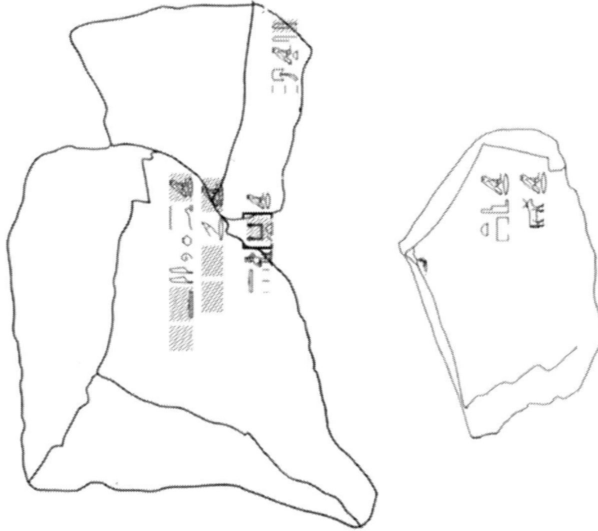

KVO 17 verso

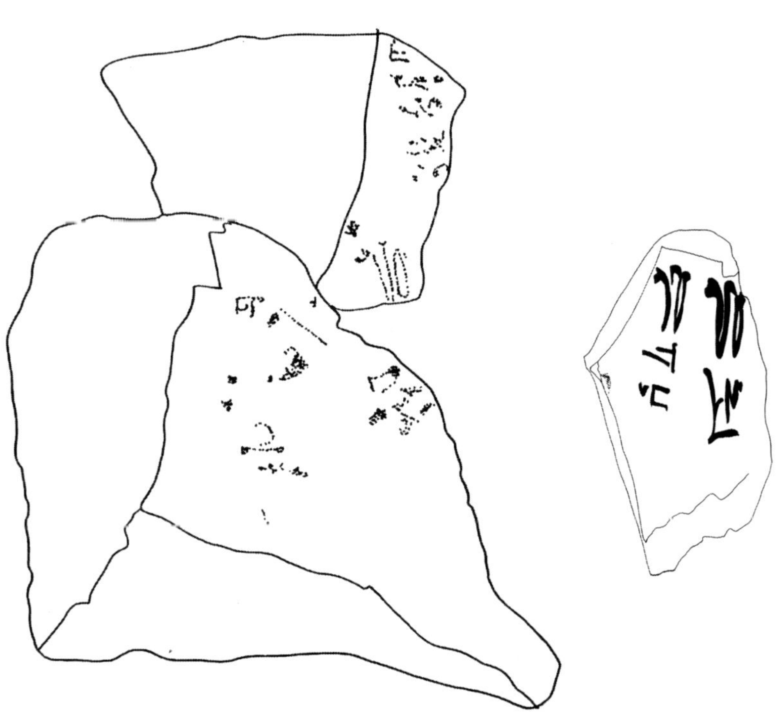

Figure 18a

KVO 18 recto

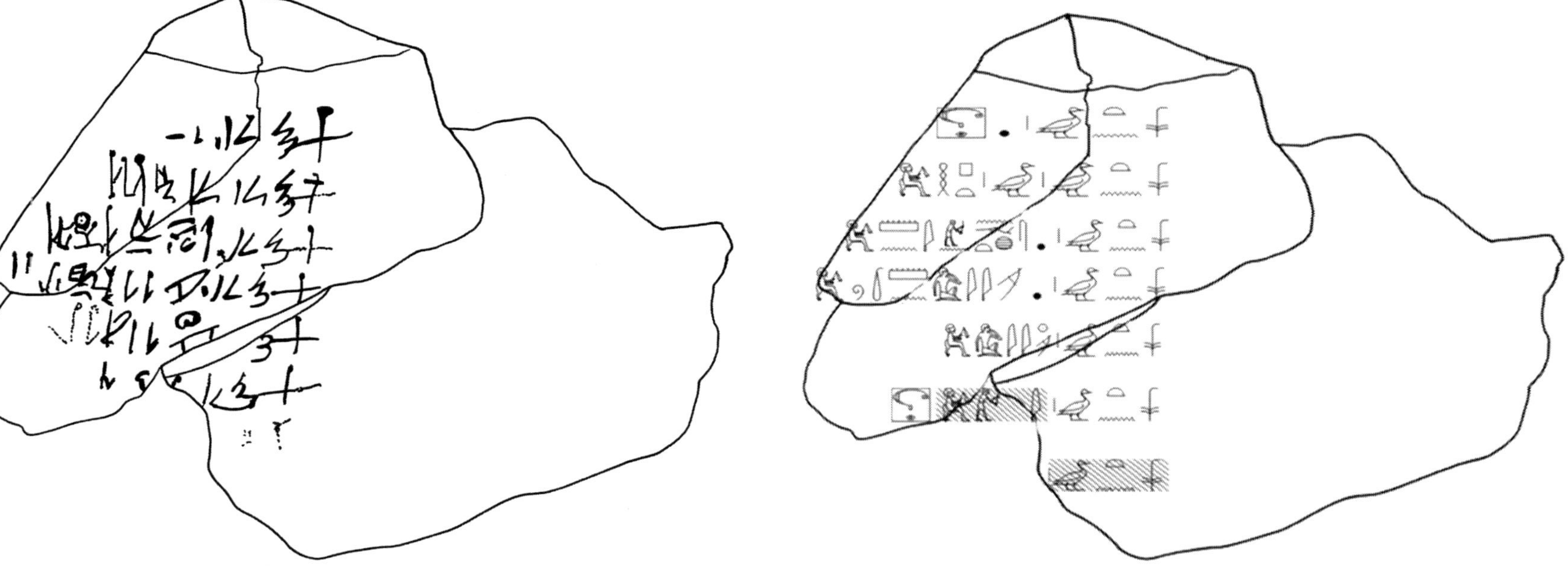

Figure 18b

KVO 18 verso

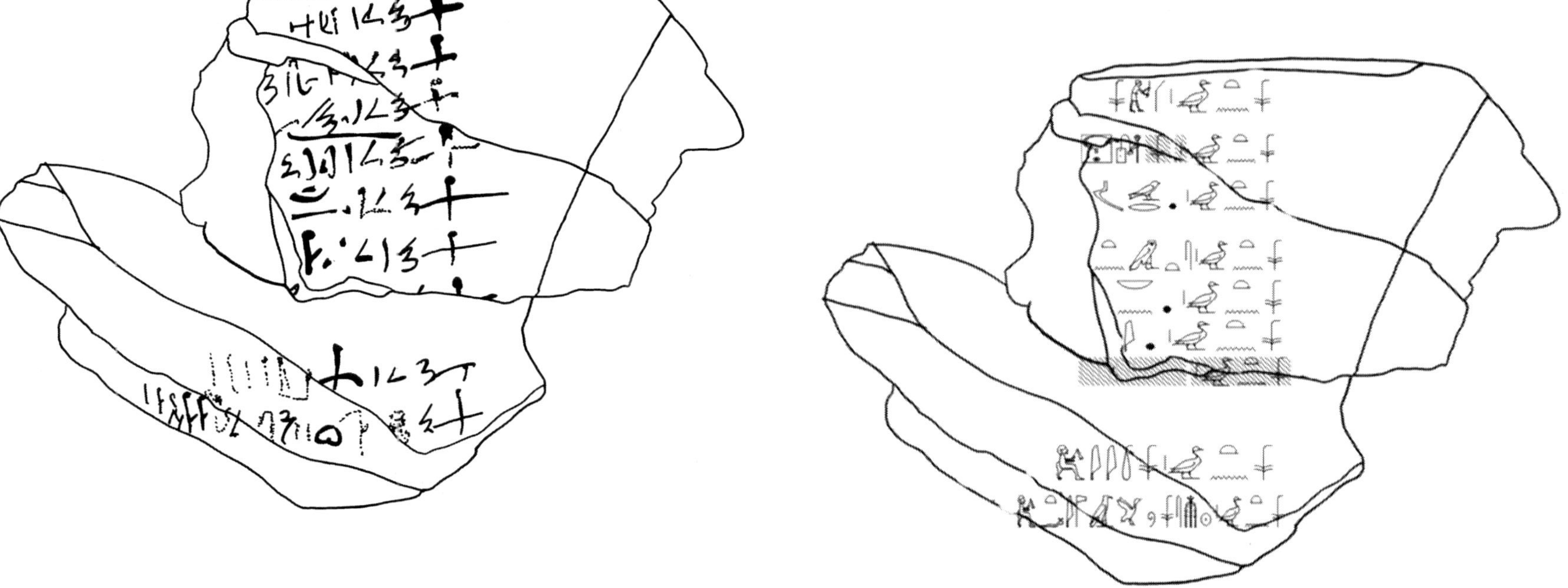

Figure 19

KVO 19

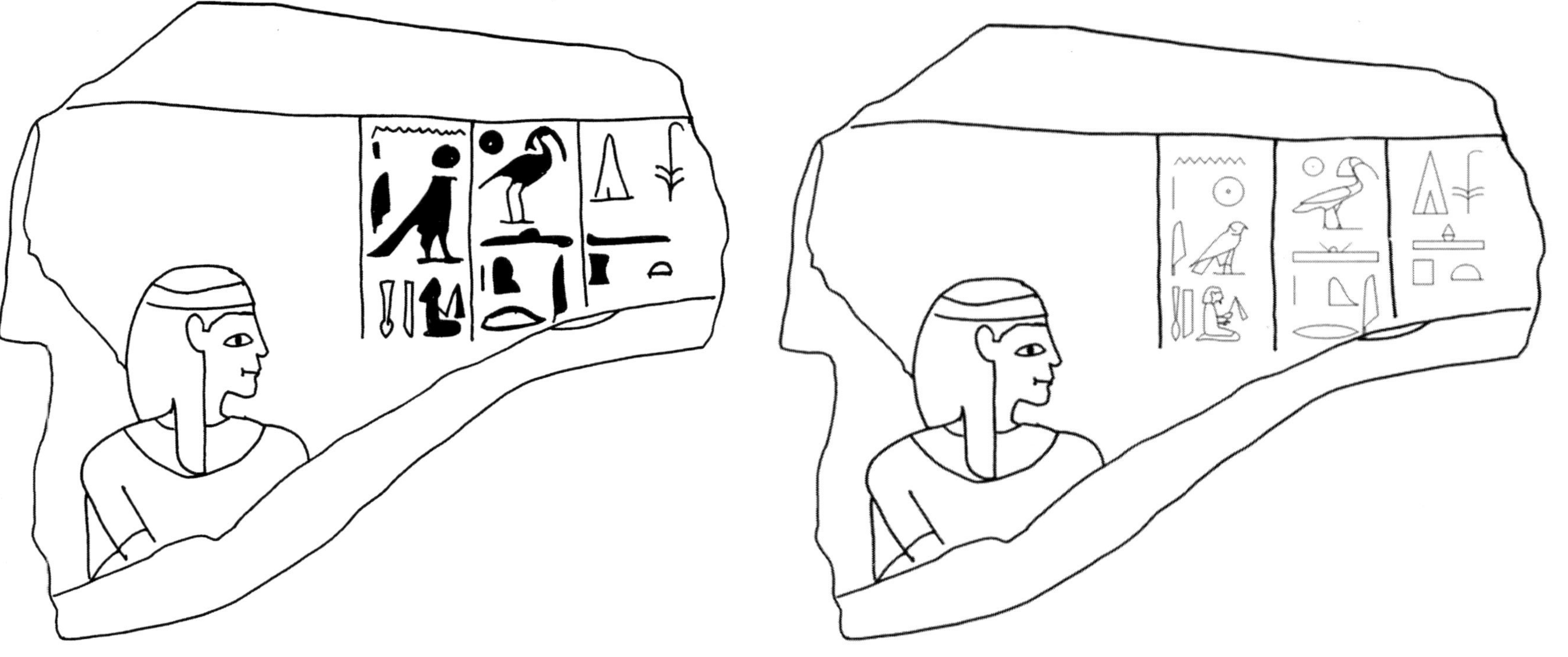

KVO 1

recto **verso**

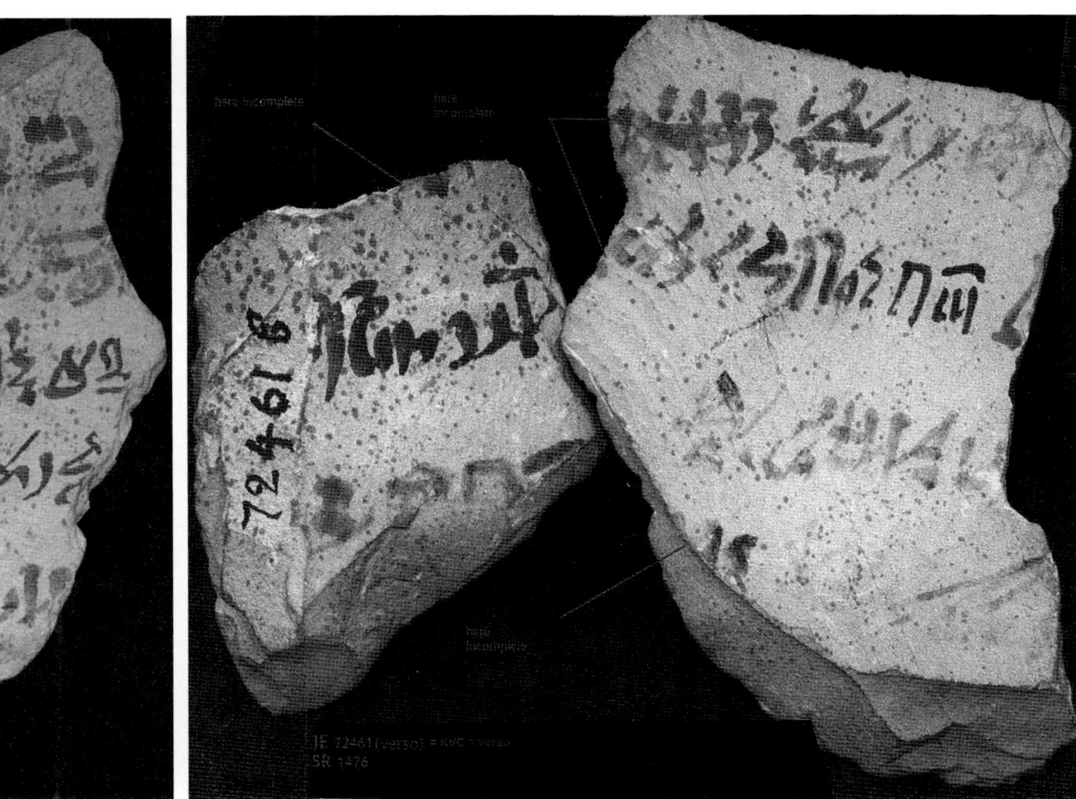

KVO 2

recto

© Cairo, Egyptian Museum

verso

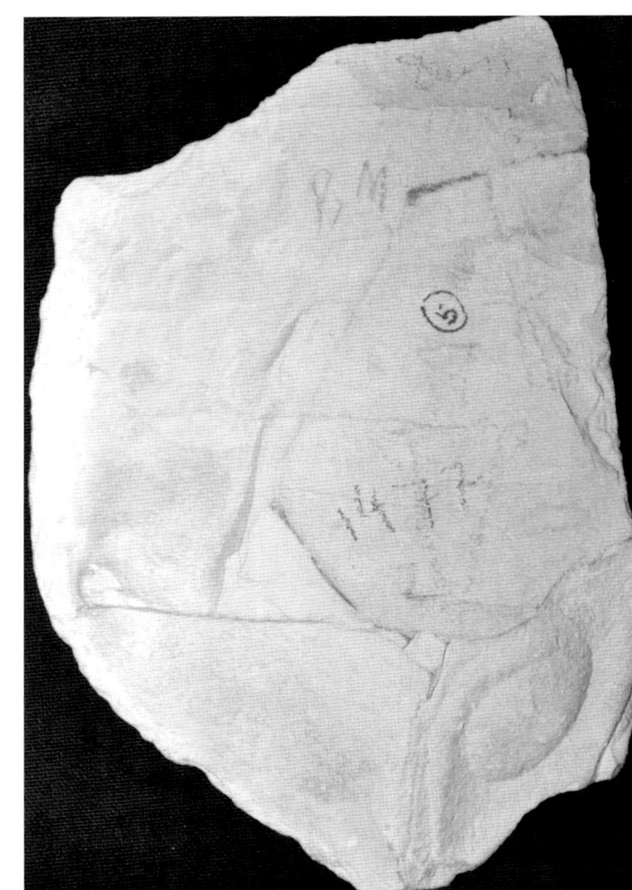

© Cairo, Egyptian Museum

KVO 3

Plate IV

KVO 4

recto

© Cairo, Egyptian Museum

verso

© Cairo, Egyptian Museum

KVO 5

recto

verso

KVO 6

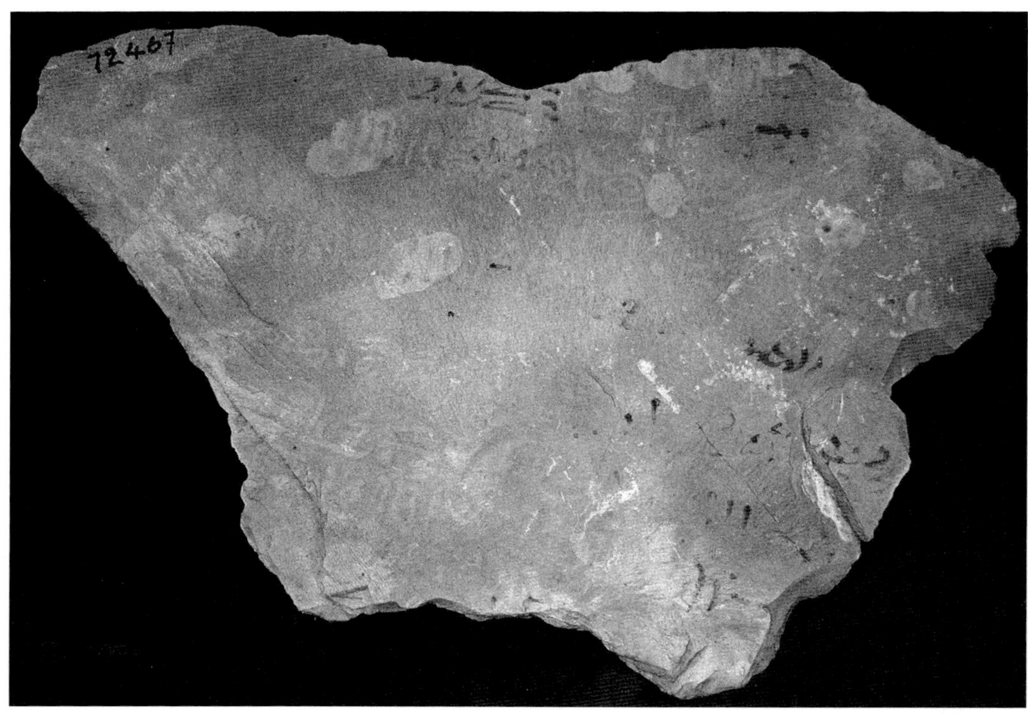

KVO 7

recto **verso**

KVO 8

recto

verso

Plate IX
KVO 9

© Cairo, Egyptian Museum

Plate X
KVO 10

© Cairo, Egyptian Museum

KVO 11

recto

verso

Plate XIII
KVO 13

Plate XIV

KVO 14

Plate XV

KVO 15

Plate XVI

KVO 16

Plate XVII

KVO 17

recto **verso**

KVO 18

recto | verso

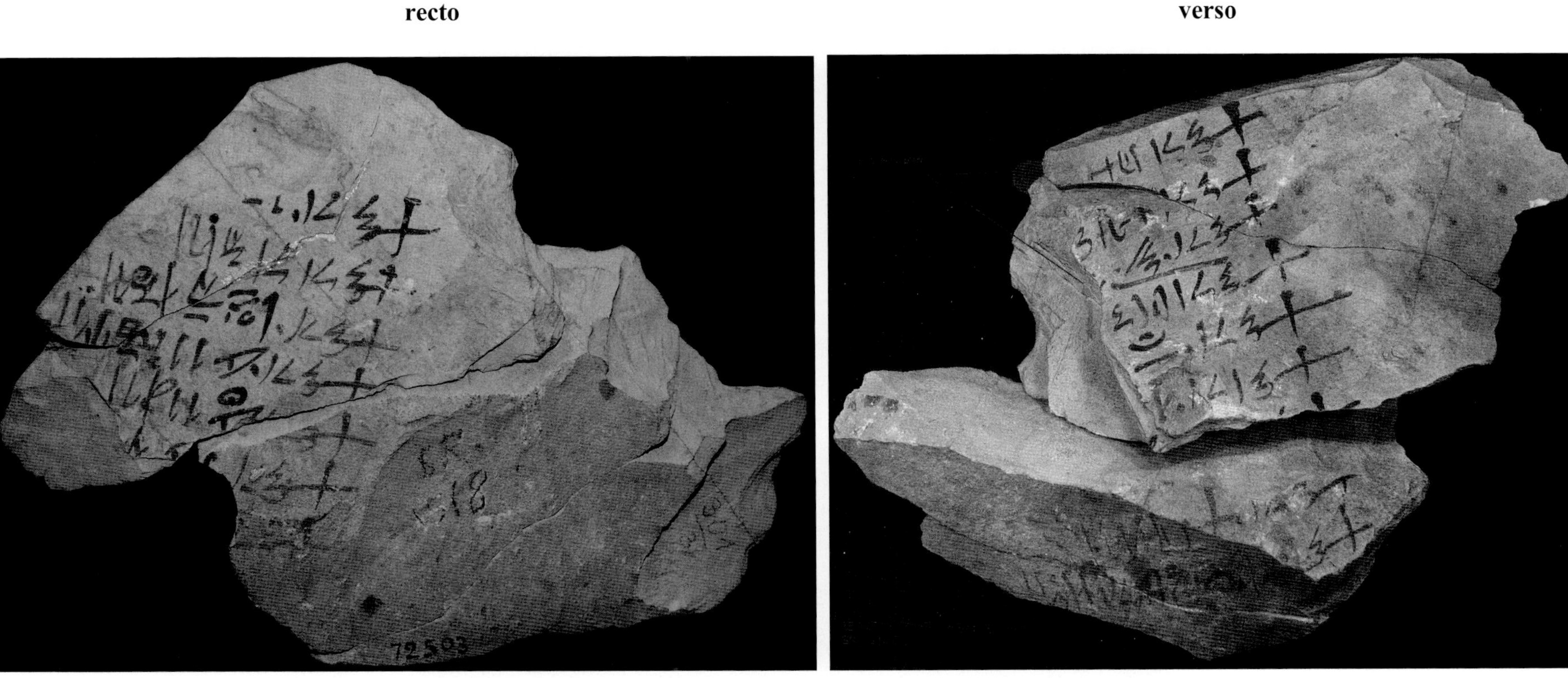

KVO 19